Golden Highlights Library

Great Castles & Palaces

Geoffrey Hindley

Camden House Books

Camden House Books
Printed and published by BPCC Publishers
Manufactured under licence from the proprietor

Created, designed and produced by
Trewin Copplestone Publishing Ltd, London

Made and printed in Great Britain by
Purnell and Sons (Book Production) Ltd.,
Member of the BPCC Group, Paulton, Bristol

ISBN 0 905015 13 4

Acknowledgments

The photographs in this book were provided by:
Aerofilms, London: 23, 29b; Lala Aufsberg: 18t, b,
19, 31, 33b, 34b, 35, 50b, 65, 66; Barnaby's Picture
Library: 53t; Bavaria Verlag: 1, 32, 39, 45t, 48, 49b,
56t, 57b, 64t, 66, 69b, 77, back cover (t); British
Museum: 24t; British Tourist Authority: 3, 7b, 8b,
9b, 10b, 12, 13, 24t, 25, 41t, 51, 79; Bulloz: 43;
Camera Press: 6, 13b; J. Allan Cash: 9t, 13t, 14, 20,
26, 63; Colour Library International: 17; Trewin
Copplestone: 56b; Photographie Giraudon: 71, 72,
73; Godfrey Goodwin: 70t, b; Sonia Halliday: 67, 68;
Michael Holford: 8t, 21, 27, 28, 40, 44, 45b, 49;
R. Hood: 33t, 34t; Victor Kennett: 58, 59t, b, 62;
A. F. Kersting: 7t, 10t, 11, 29t, 30, 38, 42, 47, 54,
56–7, 78t, 80; Emily Lane: 36; MAS: 22; Novosti
Press Agency: 55, 60t, b, 61; Picturepoint: 41b, 46,
69t, 76, 78b, back cover (b); Royal Swedish Embassy:
75t, b; Scala: 5, 52; Toni Schneiders: 50t; Spectrum:
4, 16, 37, 53b, 64b, front cover; Swiss National
Tourist Office: 15

Contents

Opposite The procession of the Knights of the Garter entering the great West Door of St George's Chapel, Windsor. Members of Europe's oldest order of chivalry, the Garter knights each have their own stalls in the choir of the Chapel with their banners hanging over them.

Pomp and pageantry

THE world's great palaces and castles are monuments of a bygone age of kings and princes; of an age when in theory, and often enough in practice, the destinies of whole peoples might be subject to the whim and power of a single man. In this book we shall visit a few of the greatest mansions, palaces and fortresses of the old world – and one in the new. Some remind us of war, some speak of past political greatness, some are grand homes, others are treasure houses of art.

Today they are for the most part massive curios, visited by tourists and studied by historians and connoisseurs of art. The magnifi-cent colorful panoply that lived in them in the days of their greatness belongs to the past. Security guards and ticket clerks have taken the place of ceremonial guards and powerful chamberlains. Instead of being conducted into a royal presence by costumed flunkies the visitor is taken on a conducted tour by uni-formed guides. But there are still palaces occupied by the successors of the rulers that built them and where the ceremonial of the past is still alive. In this chapter we discuss five such places, and we begin with one which is the residence of an autocratic ruler, which indeed is actually an independent state.

This is the **Vatican Palace** in Rome. It is bounded on one side by the huge basilica of St Peter's and the colonnade of its piazza, and the palace is encircled by walls which enclose an area of approximately one-sixth of a square mile. This is the independent state of Vatican City, set up in 1929 by the Lateran Treaty between the government of Italy and the papacy. Here the pope is absolute ruler, the last one in the western world. The state has a resident population of about 1000, but is the place of work of many more, for this is the headquarters of the Roman Catholic Church, one of the largest international organizations in the world today. The security of the territory rests with various bodies of which the most famous is the historic Swiss Guard, recruited from the Catholic Cantons. This, the personal bodyguard of the pope, was founded in 1505 by Julius II. Its colorful uniform, traditionally claimed to have been designed by Michelangelo, is a regular part of the scene at Vatican City, and the Guards play a prominent part in the ceremonies of the papal court.

The Emperor Constantine the Great built the first St Peter's in the early fourth century. It was a large basilica modeled on the administrative hall of justice of a Roman town. Two hundred years later a house was built beside the great church for distinguished visitors; the popes themselves lived at the Lateran Palace at this time. Then at the beginning of the fourteenth century a line of French popes moved the papal court to Avignon. In 1378 Gregory XI returned to Rome; finding the Lateran in ruins he took up residence at the Vatican.

The first papal election or conclave at the Vatican was held in the same year, when Gregory died. But the papacy had many troubled years ahead. The conclave elected an Italian pope, but the French party would not give up, and four astonishing decades followed during which Europe had two popes and at times even three. Some popes went in fear of their lives – one even built a passage linking the house at the Vatican to the Castle of Sant' Angelo nearby. Eventually the scandal of a divided Church was settled at the Council of Constance convened by the Emperor Sigismund in 1415. The election of Martin V two years later gave the Church a single head, but the papacy resolved that never again should a General Council have such power.

Martin and his successors set about the restoration of papal authority and the splendors of the papal court. Nicholas V (1447–55) transformed the house at the Vatican into a palace, and in 1473 Sixtus IV commanded the building of the Sistine Chapel. The popes became great patrons of the Renaissance scholars and artists, and when the ancient basilica of St Peter's showed signs of collapsing they seized the opportunity to rebuild on the magnificent scale we see today; the work took more than a century. Much other building was put in hand at the same time, but the Vatican, with its great schemes of painting, provides one of the most magnificent sights of the age.

The first of these schemes was the decoration of the Sistine Chapel, begun in 1481. The building is 133 feet long and 43 feet wide, and down each of the long sides seven frescoes depicted episodes from the lives of Christ and Moses. This work was done by such great artists as Botticelli and Pinturicchio. Then, from 1508 to 1512, Michelangelo decorated the simple barrel-vaulted ceiling with an epic series of masterpieces on themes from the book of Genesis beginning with the creation of the world. Yet more great work was still to come.

In 1534, at the command of Paul III, the great artist embarked on his majestic altarpiece of the Last Judgment. It covers the end of the chapel; before the work could be started two windows had to be walled in and two of the side wall frescoes, both by Perugino, were painted out. It is some measure of the seemingly limitless talent of Renaissance Italy that the work of such a master could be obliterated to make room for something even finer. The decoration of the series of rooms known as the Stanze and Loggia provides a still more

Opposite *Behind the great basilica of St Peter's and the walls of Vatican City lie the gardens of the papal palace.*

Below *The Sistine Chapel, looking towards Michelangelo's great masterpiece* The Last Judgment.

startling instance. Many magnificent frescoes by Perugino, Lorenzo Lotto, Piero della Francesca and others were already completed when the brilliant young Raphael Sanzio arrived in Rome. The work of his predecessors was simply blanked out and Pope Julius II gave him the sole commission to decorate the apartments throughout. Raphael's *Disputation of the Holy Sacrament* and the *School of Athens* are regarded among the purest expressions of the Renaissance spirit.

Many more great artists are represented in the picture gallery, the Pinacoteca, while the Museo Pio Clementino contains a host of famous classical sculptures, among them the renowned *Laocoön* group. The Vatican also boasts one of the world's greatest libraries, with some 60,000 rare manuscripts and hundreds of thousands of priceless printed books. Some of the most valuable treasures for the faithful of the Catholic world are housed in the Sancta Sanctorum. These are the relics of the Christian martyrs; among them are two cloaks believed to have been worn by St Peter and St John the Baptist.

The history of the papacy is a rich mixture of religious faith and scandal. Perhaps the most notorious occupant of the chair of St Peter was Alexander VI, the head of the Borgia family. The Borgia Rooms, opened to the public by Pope Leo XIII, are a suite of apartments built by Nicholas V and decorated at the commission of Pope Alexander by Pinturicchio.

The Vatican is important today because it is the center of an international administration and the home of the world's greatest museums, but the palaces and the beautiful gardens behind them remind us of its past importance, when the popes were numbered among the great powers of Europe.

Like the papacy, the English monarchy is an institution surviving from Europe's past which has lost much of its earlier power but still has considerable vitality. The Queen still lives at **Windsor**, a castle-palace that has been a residence of her predecessors for 900 years. It is in fact the oldest inhabited castle in the world and was founded by William the Conqueror. The first castle was a wooden tower on an artificial mound or *motte* surrounded by wooden palisades; it was built as a part of the chain of forts that William set up to control the defeated English. A century later Henry II decided to build in stone, and set up a Round Tower on the *motte* of the Norman castle. The lower course of masonry of the present

Round Tower dates from this period, but the rest of the structure is much more recent. The upper 30 feet of the tower and the Gothic-style battlements are part of the picturesque modifications ordered by King George IV. He also commissioned the stately private apartments in the east terrace and the magnificent south terrace with its turreted gateway. All these additions were designed by Jeffry Wyatt, a young unknown, who won the competition for the work from the famous John Nash, builder of Regent Street in London. By the time work at Windsor was finished Wyatt was a rich and fashionable architect; he received a knighthood and royal permission to change his name to Wyatville.

Wyatt was not the only architect who felt his name had been made by Windsor. After Henry II's death, his son John, who attempted to maintain his father's tough policy against the barons, faced civil war, and in 1215 was besieged at Windsor by the rebels. It was the last time that the castle was involved in warfare, but John's son Henry III made a number of additions to the fortifications. But the next great era of building at Windsor was to be directed by William of Wykeham and William of Wynford, master mason, for

Top *A dramatic shot inside the grounds of Windsor Castle. St George's Chapel is on the left and in the distance the Round Tower can be seen.*

Above *Seen from the river, Windsor is almost hidden by trees. During the middle ages the slopes would have been bare to give clear lines of fire during a siege.*

Below *The procession during the installation of new knights of the Order of the Garter at St George's Chapel in Windsor Castle.*

Bottom *The Round Tower at Windsor, seen on the right, was founded by Henry II in the twelfth century.*

Below *The procession during the installation of new knights of the Order of the Garter at St George's Chapel in Windsor Castle.*

King Edward III. Wykeham was already Master of the King's Works, but thanks to his success at Windsor, he was created Bishop of Winchester. It was clear that Windsor had made his reputation and career. The ambiguous inscription, *Hoc fecit Wykeham 1356*, still to be seen on the wall of one of the towers, can be taken to mean either "Wykeham made this" or, as King Edward angrily thought, "This made Wykeham".

Apart from the Winchester Tower and the so-called Norman Gateway, little of this fourteenth-century work survives, most of the state apartments being in the house on the north terrace, built for Charles II and his queen, Catherine of Braganza, by the architect Hugh May. But the name of King Edward III is still highly honored at Windsor as the founder, in 1346, of the famous Order of the

Bottom *The Round Tower at Windsor, seen on the right, was founded by Henry II in the twelfth century.*

Below *Architectural historians regard Buckingham Palace as a rather undistinguished building, but this winter snowscape shows it has real beauty.*

Bottom *The Changing of the Guard at Buckingham Palace is one of the most famous ceremonials in English pageantry.*

Garter, the first and now one of the last chivalric orders in Europe. The installation of Garter Knights is a brilliant and moving spectacle, led by Her Majesty the Queen as head of the Order. The home of the Order is St George's Chapel, begun in 1477 by King Edward IV and continued under his successors Richard III, Henry VII and Henry VIII.

Today, the residence of the English monarchs in their capital city of London is **Buckingham Palace.** It stands at the head of the Mall, the long low façade forming a fitting backdrop for one of the finest cityscapes in Europe, and for the statue of Queen Victoria, symbol of Britain's greatest period, which stands in a spacious circus in front of the palace. The Mall itself compares favourably with the Champs Elysées in Paris, where the long triumphal avenue culminates in the Arc de Triomphe, a

monument to military aggression; the road then continues under a different name. As a result one of the most renowned and also most clichéed features of European city design seems in reality a rather inconvenient obstruction to an urban throughway. The Mall, by contrast, leads to the town house of the constitutional head of state.

In the reign of James I the site was occupied by Goring House and the gardens were planted with mulberry trees, a measure taken to promote the domestic silk industry. In 1703 the Duke of Buckingham and Chandos built a red brick mansion on the site; in 1762 King George III bought Buckingham House for £21,000 and moved there from St James's Palace. Under his son the palace was extended and given a face lift in the form of a decorative stucco façade. During the reign of Queen Victoria the renamed Buckingham Palace underwent various modifications. For a time it had an imposing entrance arch until, in 1851, this was moved to the north end of Park Lane. It is now, as Marble Arch, a familiar landmark. The main façade of the east front was re-faced in stone in 1912, the memorial to Queen Victoria having been completed in 1911.

The state apartments are not open to the public apart from the Queen's Picture Gallery, which contains a changing collection of

Above *Four tritons support the gold State Coach, used at every English coronation since 1820. The coach, made of gilded oak, weighs four tons; on the roof are three cherubs representing England, Scotland and Ireland.*

Top *The restrained façade of Buckingham Palace is the perfect backdrop to the statue of Queen Victoria, resplendent with emblems of empire.*

Opposite *The military tattoo is one of the highlights of the annual Edinburgh Festival. Behind looms the gaunt bulk of Edinburgh Castle.*

masterpieces from the Royal Collections. In the Royal Mews can be seen the heavily opulent gold state coach, built for George III and used to carry the sovereign at every coronation since that of his son in 1820. Also in the mews (a small street which originally contained stables) is the supremely elegant Irish state coach built by M. Hutton, Lord Mayor of Dublin, in 1852.

The official residence of the monarch of the United Kingdom in her northern capital of Edinburgh is Holyrood Palace, but the historic seat of the independent Scottish kings was originally **Edinburgh Castle.** It was here that Mary Queen of Scots gave birth to a son who, as James VI of Scotland and I of England, united the two kingdoms.

For centuries the history of Edinburgh was bound up with its castle, for it lay in the disputed war zone between the English and Scots. The city takes its very name from the Anglo-Saxon king, Edwin of Northumbria – the castle was a frontier outpost of his kingdom. Over the centuries it changed hands a number of times until in 1341 Sir William Douglas secured the place for Scotland and King David II began a major re-fortification of the site. Even so, it was not until the 1450s that Edinburgh finally displaced the more northerly town of Perth as capital of Scotland.

The castle on its hill dominates the city. On three sides the land falls sharply away, while on the fourth a gentle slope forms the natural approach to the fortress. In former times it was an execution ground; today it provides a fine esplanade for the military tattoo (playing of taps) that ends the Edinburgh Festival. As the lone piper, spotlighted on the battlements, plays the lament, the world of pageantry achieves one of its most dramatic moments. The oldest part of the castle is the little chapel of St Margaret, which dates from the late eleventh or early twelfth century. It is named after the wife of King Malcolm III. Parts of the keep built by David II survive, but the bulk of the castle is sixteenth and seventeenth century. The regalia of royal Scotland is displayed in the crown room: the sword of state given by Pope Julius II to King James V, and the crown, made of Scottish gold and set with ninety-four pearls, ten diamonds and many other precious stones, remodeled for James V in 1540. One of the castle's most historic pieces is the great cannon Mons Meg. Its exact origin is uncertain but it is known to have been in use during the 1490s. Taken south to the Tower of London after the crushing of the 1745 Rebellion, it was returned to Edinburgh in the early nineteenth century at the powerful request of the great Scottish writer, Sir Walter Scott.

Below *Looking over the National Gallery of Scotland to the Castle at Edinburgh, once the chief fortress of the Kings of Scotland.*

Bottom *The famous cannons at Edinburgh Castle, and a view of the fine wooden paneling inside the building.*

Below *Caernarvon Castle, looking towards the upper bailey. In the middle ages there would have been wooden buildings in the courtyards.*

Bottom *Charles, Prince of Wales, kneels before his mother, Queen Elizabeth II, after being invested by her with the Principality of Wales at Caernarvon in July 1969.*

One of the rarest ceremonials connected with the English monarch is the installation of a Prince of Wales at the Castle of **Caernarvon.** On the last occasion, the installation of Prince Charles in 1969, the event was a great television spectacular. But, according to tradition, the first occasion was in some ways equally sensational. Edward of Caernarvon, the eldest son of Kind Edward I, was born in 1284 within the castle precincts. The king, it is said, eagerly seized on the fortuitous birth of his son amongst his enemies and took the baby on to the castle walls to present the Welsh people with a prince "who speaks no English". Later research has cast doubt on this romantic tale but, when he was seventeen, Edward was formally created Prince of Wales, and the title has been carried by the heirs apparent to the English crown since that time.

Below *Seen from across the river, Caernarvon looks like a tourist's idyll, though when it was built it was a forbidding symbol of conquest.*

Opposite *The vaulted cellars under the Castle of Chillon where François Bonivard was held prisoner for six years in the 1530s.*

The castle was one of a chain built by Edward I to consolidate his slow conquest of the last independent princes of North Wales. It was an outpost in conquered territory. The architect was a savoyard named James St George whom Edward had met on his return from the Holy Land in 1270; the ruling family of Savoy was related to his father by marriage. St George and his chief assistants, the Englishmen Walter of Hereford and Richard Lenginour, rose high in the king's favor and at the end of their lives were rich and socially established. But hundreds of lesser masons and artisans never rose above their humble station and begrudged the labor they had to spend on the king's fortresses in hostile Wales. They were recruited from the English counties from Yorkshire to Dorset and longed to be back plying their trades at home or bringing in the harvest. The building season was from April to November, the most important months of the year in an agricultural society, and the site

of a new castle had to be policed by armed horsemen to stop the workers' deserting by the score.

Almost palatial in aspect, and distinguished from all the other Welsh castles by its size, finely finished stone work, and the unusual hexagonal shape of its towers, Caernarvon was intended to serve as an administrative center for the new territories as well as a military headquarters. In fact it had a surprisingly uneventful history. During a fierce Welsh rebellion in the 1290s, the castle was overrun and its commander killed, but thereafter was virtually no trouble for the occupying forces. Within half a century the massive palace-fortress was being used primarily as a storehouse. Today, thanks to its fine state of preservation, the castle is a great tourist attraction and earns revenue for the descendants of the people it was meant to intimidate, while every two or three generations it is the setting for one of the great pageants of monarchy.

HERE we come to three castles which are famous for their romantic associations or, more simply, for their romantic appearance. Places like Chillon, in Switzerland, which delights the modern tourist with its beautiful setting and aura of legends and chivalry, were often the scenes of cruelty and injustice. They were the fortresses of privilege, and that can usually be maintained only by the exercise of power at the expense of others. The prisoner of Chillon in Byron's famous poem was no mere product of poetic imagination, he was a real man who was imprisoned in the cellars of the castle during the sixteenth century.

At that time the **Castle of Chillon** was the residence of the counts and dukes of Savoy, as it had been for centuries. It stands on an island site just off the shore of Lake Geneva near the town of Montreux, and from a distance it looks like a small town, its picturesque cluster of pinnacles and tiled roofs concealing the military strength of the place. On the landward side it is approached by a covered bridge guarded by a gatehouse. The first fortress on the island was the stone Tower of Aligne, with a protective stone wall put up in the tenth century. A hundred years later a further ring of fortifications was put up along the water's edge around the island, and a second tower, called the Tower of the Dukes, built on the northern point. This was the lord's living quarters, and other halls and apartments were gradually built around it.

In the second half of the thirteenth century, Count Peter of Savoy ordered extensive enlargements and new fortifications which gave the castle the basic appearance that it has today. The count was related by marriage to King Henry III of England, and he took advantage of this to make a name and position for himself there. The king created him Earl of Richmond and presented him with a palace on a site now occupied by the Savoy Hotel in London.

Chillon was a favorite residence for Count Peter and many of his successors. The chief apartment in the Tower of the Dukes is the *camera domini* or Lord's Hall. Its walls were embellished for the dukes by Italian and French painters. Faded wall paintings can still be seen depicting scenes from hunting or stories from old legends. Over the fireplace St George is shown impaling the dragon, while on the other walls we can trace the outlines of bull and lion and even the exotic camel, antelope and leopard. This was the main living room; adjoining it was a small chamber that led into the great hall now called the Hall of the Knights. It has a fine barrel-vaulted ceiling, and there are splendid views of the lake from its windows. Below this was the public Great Hall where the ruler entertained his guests of honor and held court among his subjects and tenantry.

Both these halls were built for Count Peter though there have been numerous alterations and additions since his time. Most notable of these is the sixteenth-century paneled ceiling in the Great Hall. Another fine room was reserved for the castellan, the officer who was in charge in the absence of the ruler. Below are the fine vaulted cellars. They are very similar to the underground stables at the Castle of the Counts at Ghent, Belgium, and may originally have been intended to serve the same purpose. However, they came to be used as a prison, and it was here that François Bonivard, the "prisoner of Chillon", passed six years in confinement.

This alone would entitle him to our sympathy. Although the cellars are not below the surface of the lake as he claimed – indeed they

look out over its waters – they are cold and dank and must have been a terrible place during winter. Tradition has it that Bonivard was chained to the third pillar from the door throughout the six years, and Byron at least seems to have accepted the legend for he carved his name on that pillar. But the famous prisoner was not quite the simple and noble patriot of the poet's imagination. He was imprisoned for siding with the citizens of Geneva in their struggle to throw off the rule of Duke Charles III of Savoy, but he had first fallen out with the ducal government while defending the rights of the Abbey of St Victor where he was a monk. Released after this first brush with authority, he seems to have tried to keep out of harm's way, but had the bad luck to be captured by a gang of highwaymen who handed him over to the authorities to curry favor with the duke. When the castle was finally captured by the victorious forces of Geneva and Berne in 1536, Bonivard was brought back as a hero to Geneva. He was given a place on the governing council and was even asked to write a history of the city.

The romance of **Neuschwanstein** in Bavaria is of recent vintage compared with Chillon, dating as it does from the nineteenth century. For 112 years Bavaria enjoyed the status of an independent kingdom. The title was awarded by Napoleon in 1806 to the Elector Maximilian, but the elector was shrewd enough to desert the French just before their defeat at Leipzig in 1813, and thus retained his territory virtually intact after the new settlement of Europe drawn up by the Congress of Vienna. His successors were to prove prodigal spenders and liberal patrons of the arts; from King Ludwig II (1846–86) onwards they also showed a disturbing tendency to go mad.

Ludwig succeeded to his father Maximilian II in 1864. The auguries were good: he was young and handsome and the son of a king noted for his liberalism in politics and generosity as a patron. Ludwig was also undeniably talented. In the first year of his reign he called the composer Richard Wagner to court. The young monarch was spell-bound by the strength of the composer's personality and bemused by the semi-mystical pretensions of his operas. He planned to finance both man and music – and well beyond the resources of his kingdom. His ministers, backed by public opinion, forced the king to relinquish his protégé, and Wagner left Bavaria in 1865; yet

King Ludwig II of Bavaria wanted to build a dream castle at Neuschwanstein. This quite breathtaking picture shows how well he succeeded.

ten years later the Wagner Festival Theater was built on Bavarian soil at Bayreuth thanks largely to a loan guaranteed by the king.

Ludwig's fevered imagination was in love with the middle ages, when chivalry lived in Germany and Germany was a great power in Europe. In 1869 he began the building of an ideal dream castle near Hohenschwangau, overlooking the Schwanensee. He wrote ecstatically to Wagner, "The site is one of the most beautiful imaginable; it is sacred and it is inaccessible." He was right on the second point at least; even today the tourist in quest of photographs soon realizes that the best shots are to be had only from the air. Most of his time Ludwig seems to have lived in a world of make-believe but, being a king, he was able to make the beliefs come more true than most people. Accordingly when designing his castle he went first not to an architect, but to a painter-stage designer.

The result is a cluster of fairy-tale towers and turrets that spring up from the craggy sides of the Bertzenkopf, high above the gorge of the Pöllat River. Indeed, this astonishing folly is a riot of medieval and Wagnerian fantasy. The king's study is decorated with scenes from *Tannhäuser* and leads off to a room in the shape of a grotto, also taken from that legend. The bathroom suite has scenes from the poems of the thirteenth-century troubadour or Minnesänger, Walther von der Wogelweide and one from the story of the Master Singers. In the bedroom it is the story of Tristan and Yseult from Gottfried von Strassburg. The dining room has the portraits of other Minnesänger and of the Landgrave Herman of Hesse who held a great poetry and song contest at his castle in the Wartburg in the early thirteenth century. Neuschwanstein boasts, too, a *Sängersaal* or Singers' Hall copied from the room in the Wartburg Castle where that historic contest is thought to have taken place; there is furniture carefully copied from pieces in the Wartburg. The chapel takes for its theme St Louis IX, King of France, whom Ludwig had adopted as his personal patron saint. But the royal fantasy reached its height in the throne room. Running the length of one wing it is two stories high, and the decorative theme tells the story of Lohengrin, the Knight of the Swan and the subject of Wagner's opera of the same name. Literally, Neuschwanstein means the "New Castle of the Swan"–the king liked to identify himself with Lohengrin. His ideal of kingship is indicated by the fact that the frescoes round

Bottom opposite *King Ludwig II's bedroom in Neuschwanstein. The riot of decoration, Gothic in inspiration, was far wilder than any medieval king could have dreamed of.*

Below *The courtyard seen from Ludwig's apartment. Despite the pinnacles and polygonal towers which are copied from late medieval styles, the Romanesque colonnading creates a strong and convincing effect.*

Right *The famous Alcazar of Segovia seen from the valley to the north; the rivers Eresma and Clamores flow together at the foot of the rock.*

Left *The Tower of King John II who, with his son and successor, built much of the Alcazar in the fifteenth century.*

the apse in which stands the throne are portraits of six medieval monarchs canonized by the Catholic church.

Ludwig's eccentricities were extravagant rather than dangerous, but the money he played with came from taxpayers. It was inevitable that he would be relieved of his throne sooner or later; it is only surprising that he lasted so long. However, in 1886, a committee duly declared him insane and news of his deposition was sent to Neuschwanstein where he was in residence; he was taken to the castle at Sternbergersee where he was kept under medical supervision. On 13 June 1886 his body was found in the lake in circumstances suggesting suicide. Neuschwanstein is not the only castle that he built, but it is the most remarkable monument of a king who for twenty-two glorious years played at chivalry in the midst of the harshly practical nineteenth century. One cannot avoid a certain respect for the man.

The famous **Alcazar of Segovia** seems to sail like a great galleon across the landscape of Castile. It is situated on a spur of land at the junction of the rivers Eresma and Clamores, and from the prow of this land-locked ship the terrain falls sharply away into the valley. The town of Segovia was important in Roman times, and the site of the castle, which had been fortified by the Visigoth conquerors of Spain in the early middle ages, was strengthened still further by the Muslims.

During the eighth century Muslim armies from North Africa overran almost the entire Spanish peninsula, and it took the Christian princes seven centuries to drive the last representatives of Islam from their territories. During the eleventh century the caliphs of Cordoba fortified the castle in an attempt to

Right *The throne room at the Alcazar, Segovia. In the frieze the coats of arms of the Christian monarchs alternate with abstract pierced designs of obviously Moorish influence.*

Opposite *The imposing scale of the fortifications of London's Tower of London can best be appreciated in an aerial photograph. The rings of walls and moat make it an almost copy-book example of a "concentric" castle, though they are in fact the result of various periods of building.*

stem the advance of Christian reconquest, but in 1083 it fell to the forces of King Alfonso VI of Leon and Castile. Yet the very name of the fortress, Alcazar, is an Arabic word, reminding us of its checkered history. Alfonso and his successors kept the fortifications in good repair and added to them still further. But the palace that we see today dates mostly from the fifteenth century and is the work of King John II of Castile and his son and successor Henry IV.

The poop of the fortress-galleon of Segovia is formed by the Tower of John II with its hanging turrets and decorative brickwork, so typical of Castilian architecture of this period. The rooms of the castle tell the familiar story of transition from fortress to palace. The Salon de la Galera is decorated with a frieze designed by Muslim artists converted to Christianity and showing the characteristic blend of Islamic and Christian styles known as *mudejar*. It was done for Queen Catherine, the daughter of the English Duke of Lancaster, John of Gaunt.

The room known as the Pieza del Cordon is associated by tradition with Alfonso X, called the Wise. On one occasion he uttered the blasphemous remark that had he been the creator the universe would have been ruled better – a view not confined to medieval monarchs. That night, it is said, a terrible storm broke over the castle and a thunderbolt hurtled into the royal chamber. The storm did not clear until the king begged forgiveness for his pride.

THE **Tower of London** has been the chief fortress of the English monarchy for 900 years. Today it is garrisoned by a regiment of the regular British Army, being the headquarters of the Royal Fusiliers, and as the repository of the crown jewels is still important as a stronghold. Additions have been made in every century except the fifteenth so that the Tower is now one of the most extensive as well as one of the best-preserved castles in Europe.

The name comes from the great central White Tower, built by William the Conqueror in the late 1070s. Within months of entering his new capital the victorious king had built a wooden fortress protected to the east by the ancient Roman wall of London. The new stone tower was built under the direction of Gundulf of Bec, who later became bishop of Rochester where he built a castle for himself very like the White Tower. The original entrance, like that at Rochester and many other eleventh-century stone keeps, was on the first floor and reached by a wooden stairway. If the castle were to be attacked the staircase could easily be knocked away or burnt down so that the attackers could not reach the main door. The entrance has for long been at ground floor level and, another change, many of the original Norman windows were altered to their present classical design during the seventeenth century.

Otherwise the White Tower looks much the same today as when it was finished. It is about 90 feet high and some 110 feet square; it is divided down the center by a massive stone wall, running from floor to ceiling and dividing the tower into two compartments. If one were overrun by an attacker the garrison could retreat to the other and continue resistance. On the west side there is the Council Room on the top floor and the banqueting hall below it; these now house parts of the Tower's superb collection of armor. The finest part of the White Tower is the Chapel of St John which occupies the two upper floors of the southeast corner of the keep. It is one of the best-preserved examples of Norman architecture in England.

The White Tower was completed by the Conqueror's son, William Rufus. For a century it stood guard over the capital, one of the strongest fortresses in the kingdom. Then King Richard I, the greatest of medieval military architects, began a series of alterations and additions which over the next two centuries transformed the austere tower into a copy-book example of a "concentric" castle, ringed about with walls and towers. The outermost defenses on the west, north and east sides were provided by a moat, and on the south the river Thames completed the circuit; later on in the middle ages a wharf was built along the river front, and the southern wall of the tower was protected by a continuation of the moat. Access to the tower from the river was through a heavily protected gate – many a distinguished prisoner passed under its gloomy arch to await trial for treason.

The long list of state prisoners stretches from Ranulf Flambard, the unpopular minister of William Rufus, to Rudolf Hess. As chief minister Flambard must have authorized the expenditure on completion of the White Tower, so it is ironical that in 1100, the year of his master's death, he was imprisoned there for a time, indeed he is the first man recorded as a prisoner in the fortress. Hess was lodged there in May 1941 immediately after his defection from Hitler's Germany.

He was driven in by car, but for centuries enemies of the state and monarch had been brought to the Tower by water and entered through Traitors' Gate. Among them was the young Princess Elizabeth, later to be queen, imprisoned by order of her sister Mary I. Years later Elizabeth herself was forced to condemn her rebellious favorite, the Earl of Essex, to await his execution in the Tower, while in the next reign the great Sir Walter Raleigh languished there to satisfy the spite of James I, King of England

Top opposite *This view of the Tower comes from an edition of the poems of Duke Charles of Orleans, seen leaning out of the window.*

Bottom opposite *St John's Chapel, occupying the first and second floors of the south-east corner of the White Tower, is among the best-preserved of Norman buildings.*

Below *The decorative uniforms of the Yeoman Warders of the Tower look almost out of place under the glowering arch of Traitors' Gate.*

In 1671, the Tower witnessed a dangerous, dramatic and nearly successful attempt to steal the crown jewels. It was organized by a certain Captain Blood. Disguised as a minister he first reconnoitred the ground and won the trust of the keeper of the Jewel House; then one night he and two accomplices overpowered the guard and succeeded in getting the crown, orb and scepter. Blood hid the crown under his cloak, another pocketed the orb while a third began to saw the scepter in half. But the keeper's son had rallied help and the three robbers were taken. The fact that King Charles II almost immediately pardoned Blood and in addition granted him a state pension and lands in Ireland has led to the not unreasonable assumption that the penniless if merry monarch may have had a hand in this attempt on the state crown jewels.

Today they are one of the main attractions for visitors to the Tower. The regalia used at coronations form the centerpiece of the collection. Apart from the medieval spoon and ampule used for anointing the head of the monarch with holy oil, they all date from the late seventeenth century, made for Charles II himself, on his restoration to the throne. The bulk of the medieval regalia was sold during the Commonwealth, England's brief and early experiment as a republic.

In former times the Tower of London, a great gaunt bastion on the outskirts of London, was a place of evil reputation; today it is surrounded by busy streets and offices, and Tower Green, the site of many executions, is merely a place of antiquarian interest. The uniforms of the Yeoman Warders make a colorful display for tourists, but when founded in the early sixteenth century these soldiers were a stern and dangerous body of men. King Henry VII, who acknowledged that he had no legal right to the throne, was also the first English king to have a personal bodyguard. The Yeoman of the Guard and the Yeoman Warders of the Tower had a deadly serious job to do.

Legend has it that the Tower will not fall until the ravens stop nesting there. They have their quarters in a cage on the Lanthorn Tower and must surely be among the best-cared for birds in London.

Despite the romance that hangs around his name, King Richard I cared little for England. He spent less than a year there during the whole of his reign, and seems to have regarded his kingdom as a mere source of revenue to finance his campaigning first on the Crusades and then in northern France, defending the lands of his family in Normandy against the French King Philip Augustus. As a king he had little to recommend him, as a soldier and military architect he was outstanding. His work on the Tower in London was completely outshone by **Château Gaillard** in France, a masterpiece of castle design.

Today it is a mighty ruin. The lofty cliff on which it stands towers over the little town of Les Andelys on a bend of the Seine, fifty miles north-west of Paris. It was to guard the approaches to the English duchy of Normandy, and Richard called it his "Saucy

Castle". With it he dared the French to conquer the territory which for centuries had been independent of the French crown.

In the planning stages Richard had to face protests from the Archbishop of Rouen, head of the church in Normandy, who owned the land. According to tradition God intervened and heaven itself "rained blood"; the local people were convinced that even had he sent an angel to put a stop to the building, the king would have sent him packing with a curse. Richard came from a wild and arrogant family, and was determined to finish the fortress so important to his military schemes. In fact he did pay compensation to the church, but, by then the castle was nearly completed.

It stands at the end of a jutting promontory and can be approached from only one side, guarded by an 'outer bailey' or walled court-yard. An attacking force, unless it was prepared to battle up the ravines that surrounded the castle proper, had first to take this bailey and then cross the precipitous ditch that separated it from the double line of fortifications sur-rounding the great keep or *donjon*. The place was strong and the garrison was loyal, even to King John who succeeded his brother Richard; yet Château Gaillard remained in English hands barely ten years.

In 1203 King Philip Augustus of France determined to take it—by starvation. He built a ring of walls and ditches around the place just out of bow shot from the walls and prepared to besiege the isolated garrison. His soldiers jeered up at the English, locked up in their mountain eyrie "like so many baby eagles that would be forced to try to fly when the spring came". The civilians who had taken refuge in the castle soon had to be driven out to conserve the supplies for the fighting men, and when the French refused them passage through their lines they were forced to starve under the castle walls. There were many cases of cannibalism. In the spring, King Philip ordered the attack. Things went slowly until an ingenious French soldier called, we are told, Peter Snub Nose, discovered a way up inside the drains and with a small party of men took the defenders by surprise. They attempted to drive back the enemy by setting fire to the wooden outbuild-

ings, but the conflagration spread through the whole castle, and despite a heroic defense it fell to the French. Within a year the whole of Normandy was lost.

Castles were often so strong that it was almost impossible to take them by direct assault. Such a place was **Krak des Chevaliers**, the great Crusader fortress in Palestine, brilliantly designed, massively built and provisioned for a year or more, virtually impregnable. It belonged to the Knights Hospitaller, an order which had been founded at the beginning of the eleventh century to look after sick pilgrims in Jerusalem. Before long the knights extended their duties to protecting the pilgrims en route by force of arms.

Opposite *The gaunt ruin of Château Gaillard still breathes something of its military past. In the background is the bend of the Seine on which the castle stands.*

Top *Krak des Chevaliers from the south-west showing the aqueduct and the square tower added by Krak's Islamic conquerors. Behind the walls rises the great* talus *surrounding the central fortress.*

Above *Krak des Chevaliers from the air. The inner wall is protected by a massive* talus *of projecting masonry; half way along it the chapel projects to form an additional tower for the defenders.*

29

Krak, which defends the route from the coastal Christian cities to the Islamic stronghold of Homs, is designed in two massive rings of walls around the crest of a little hill. These are strengthened by projecting towers, and the chief living quarters are within the inner ring. The weakest part of the site is to the south where the hill slopes away gently. Here the inner wall, dominated by three towers, was protected at its base by a masonry skirt or *talus* that plunges outwards and downwards to a depth of 30 feet. Spreading out like this made it almost impossible for attackers to sap the foundations of the wall, and scaling the smooth hard stone of the *talus* itself was equally difficult. Even to reach the inner wall an outer fortification had to be breached and then a deep reservoir, or *berquil*, had to be crossed. The main entrance lay to the east; it was nothing less than a death trap. The route from the outer gateway was up a zig-zag ramp which was roofed over. Unexpected openings to the sides offered vantage points for surprise attacks to the defending troops while boiling pitch could be poured down on the attacking enemy from holes in the roof. Everywhere in the great defenses we find evidence of the architect's skill, while vast storage cellars could house supplies for a 2000-man garrison for the space of a year.

Nevertheless Krak des Chevaliers fell. It was in 1271. The Christian position in Palestine as a whole was virtually lost when the Sultan Baibars launched his first attack on Krak the morning of March 3. After a month, a breach had been made in the southern outer wall. Seeing the *berquil* and impressive inner defenses, the sultan realized that the garrison could hold out for months, and resorted to trickery. A renegade Christian in the Muslim camp forged a letter which ordered the commander of the castle to surrender, on the authority of the Grand Master of the Order of the Hospital. The message was sent by carrier pigeon over the walls.

No doubt the commander detected the forgery; he also knew that his long-term position was hopeless. The Christians were being driven out of Palestine and no one would come to relieve him. He ordered his men to surrender, using the letter to justify his decision. Like many another great castle Krak fell not because of its structural or design weakness but because of the poor morale of its defenders. The architect could build an impregnable fortress, but he could not ensure the fighting spirit of the men whose job it was to defend it.

Princes and patrons

PALACES were by no means the preserve of royalty. In this chapter we look at four great residences whose builders did not boast kingly crowns. One was built by a great merchant family, one by a prince of the Church, one by a prince of the Holy Roman Empire, and one by a national English hero.

The Venice of today is a magnificent city. It was once the capital of Europe's first great maritime empire. In the fifth century, barbarians invading the Roman Empire forced hundreds of refugees to seek security on a group of islands and mud flats at the head of the Adriatic Sea. Gradually they organized themselves as an embryo state under a doge (from the Latin word, *dux* meaning "leader"). Later

the Franks forced them still further into their island refuge and they established their headquarters on the island of Rialto. It was here that the first Doge's Palace began to rise in the early years of the ninth century.

At first the sea had given Venice protection, but now it was offering the road to wealth. Venetian seamen and merchants began to establish their trading stations and fortresses down the Dalmatian coast, and soon they were pushing into the Aegean and even the Black Sea. Here they came sharply into contact with the Byzantine Empire, based on Constantinople and, in rivalry with other Italian trading cities such as Pisa and Genoa, competed for the control of its rich trade.

In this fine view of old Venice (below) *we can see the domes of the cathedral of St Marks rising behind the lagoon façade of the Doge's Palace.*

The illustration (bottom) *shows the Porta della Carta in the courtyard of the Doge's Palace, and* (opposite) *is the Piazza of St Mark's after a flood, with the Doge's Palace on the right.*

Venice's navy became a major factor in Mediterranean affairs and eventually enabled her to divert even the Crusading movement to serve her interests. When in 1202 the leaders of the so-called Fourth Crusade were looking for transport to take them to the Holy Land they found the Fleet of Venice offering its services. To pay their passage they had only to sail first to Constantinople to help the city establish its position there. For Venice the notorious expedition was a success. The Crusaders never fought a single Muslim army, but they did sack Christian Constantinople (1204) and divided the spoils with the merchants of Venice.

In the centuries that followed, the Venetians built up an island empire in former Byzantine territories and even withstood the Turks who finally overran the Empire in 1453. However, the discovery of new trade routes during the fifteenth and sixteenth centuries slowly undermined Venice's position, though her magnificence for long continued to dazzle Europe. During the eighteenth century her decline became apparent, and when Napoleon entered the city in 1797 she yielded her independence without a fight.

The present **Doge's Palace** was begun in

the 1340s. The first part to be built was the wing overlooking the Molo or Lagoon quay. the work was slowed down by the Black Death of 1347 and wars with Genoa but was at last completed in 1407 with the decorative balcony in the center of the façade. This façade is almost unique in western architecture. Two ranges of open arches, forming a colonnade on the ground floor with a fantastically colonnaded balcony above, are surmounted by a high smooth wall picked out in geometric patterns. The Venetians themselves were so delighted with the effect that they decided to duplicate it with another wing to overlook the Piazzetta.

At the corner are carvings showing Adam and Eve, and above them the archangel Michael overcoming the devil. Numerous other carvings in the capitals of the pillars on the façade overlooking the Piazzetta include personifications of the Virtues and the Vices; the Childhood of Man; and representations of the planets and constellations. One sculpture shows the city personified as Justice flanked by lions tearing the representations of military and civil rebellion limb from limb. It seems the city fathers had an educational, not to say propagandist, motive in commissioning the subjects for the sculptors.

Within the palace, art and history jostle for the visitor's attention. At the focus of the main courtyard stands the Foscari Arch; it carries a statue of the doge whose name it bears and is adorned with other statues and pinnacles. It was in this courtyard that another doge, the ill-fated Marino Falieri, was murdered on a staircase since destroyed. He was charged with treason because he joined a popular revolt against the oppressive power of the merchant aristocrats although he was himself a member of the class. Falieri's death in 1355 marked the last of the few occasions in Venetian history when the common people tried to assert their rights, and in the fifteenth century, the election of Doge Francesco Foscari was the last occasion on which the formula announcing a new doge included a mention of the people as playing any part in the proceedings at all.

It was at the head of the Staircase of the Giants that a new doge traditionally received the strangely shaped cap of office. The staircase gets its name from the colossal figures of Neptune and Mars carved by Jacopo Sansovino in 1554; they symbolize Venice's claim to supremacy at sea and in land warfare. The principal access to the palace is the Staircase of Gold, once reserved for ambassadors and city magistrates. The doge's private apartments are on the second floor, and below them is the room containing the so-called Book of Gold in which the children of the aristocracy had to be registered at birth. The government of the city was confined to the great families, but not even they could take part if their nobility were not vouched for by their registration in the Book of Gold.

Above the doge's suite were the chief rooms of state, of which the largest was the Sala del Maggior Consiglio, the Hall of the Great Council. It is 180 feet in length; the walls and ceiling are decorated with scenes from Venetian history, while around the frieze are the portraits of the first seventy-six doges—all except Mario Falieri whose name and crime against the oligarchy are alone recorded. The room is dominated by a vast painting by Tintoretto, claimed to be the largest canvas painting in the world, which takes a scene from Dante's poem *Paradiso* as its theme. The Great Council was great only in name, the real power lay with a much smaller body. During the fifteenth century, the doge himself became little more than a figurehead, though he continued to preside over the cabinet meetings in the Sala del Collegio. Here too there are fine paintings by Tintoretto, though the whole of

Bottom opposite *The carvings of Adam and Eve at the corner of the façades of the Doge's Palace were carved about 1425.*

Below *The Bridge of Sighs, over which prisoners passed from the court in the palace to their imprisonment.*

one wall is given over to a depiction of the great naval victory Venice won over the Turks at Lepanto in 1571; this masterpiece is by Paolo Veronese.

The most feared of all Venetian government bodies was the Council of Ten. It held its meetings in a small room near the cabinet chamber, and from thence many state prisoners, often merely personal enemies of the councillors, were sent to imprisonment in the cells under the lead roof of the palace. When a separate prison was eventually built, the way from the council room in the palace led over the famous Bridge of Sighs; the cells were still called "the Leads"

Some twenty miles to the east of Rome, the little town of Tivoli climbs a hillside that looks out over the eternal city to the sea beyond. The district was to become a favorite one for the out-of-town villas of wealthy Romans, but when in 1550 the architect Pirro Ligorio began to prepare his plans for the **Villa d'Este**, the fashion for the place had barely begun. There were only the ruins of ancient Roman villas, such as the one built for the Emperor Hadrian, to recall the popularity Tivoli had enjoyed in classical times.

Ligorio had been commissioned by Cardinal Ippolito d'Este, the papal governor of the town and one of the leading princes of the Church,

who was ambitious for the papal throne. The
cardinal came from one of Italy's oldest
princely houses. On his father's side the house
of Este traced descent back to the early tenth
century, while through his mother, Lucretia
Borgia, he could claim even a pope, Alexander
VI, for his grandfather. He was just over forty-
one when his grand new villa began to rise. It
took ten years to build and was to become one
of the most celebrated villas in Italy.

Even for an Italian prince Ippolito d'Este
was a great patron of the arts. The decorations
of the house took more than twenty years to
complete and were executed by Girolamo
Muziano, later superintendant of the works at

*Above The Fountain of the Organ at the
Villa d'Este. It and the Neptune Fountain make
up a grand composition of falling sheets of water
and jets rising from different levels.*

*Opposite The Villa d'Este is a somewhat austere
building, but its gardens and fountains make it one
of the most enchanting palaces in Europe. Here
we show the "Rometta" fountain.*

the Vatican, and Federico Zuccaro, who spent a year in the 1570s at the court of Queen Elizabeth I of England. Scores of lesser men also worked on the decorations. For centuries the villa housed one of the most important collections of classical sculpture ever assembled, and today it is an Italian state museum.

Even in Italy, where the art of the formal garden evolved during the Renaissance, the gardens of the Villa d'Este are renowned. During the middle ages there had been fish ponds on the site, and these were retained in a scheme where water played a major role. They were redesigned as ornamental lakes with artificial islands on which were built pleasure pavilions; elaborate waterworks were an essential part of Italian garden design. Lying on the hillside the gardens are laid out in rising ter-

races. The paths are dappled by the sunlight glancing through the evergreen ilex trees and all about is the sound of water playing. The most beautiful part of the gardens is the terrace of a hundred fountains which stretch for the whole length of one of the spacious walks. Compared with the luxuriance and grace of the gardens the house is somewhat austere in style, yet the overall effect of this pleasure palace, built for a prince of the Church, is one of elegance and rich charm.

The palace of **Nymphenburg**, lying on the outskirts of Munich in Bavaria, is on a more grandiose scale. It was begun in 1664 by the Electress Henrietta Adelaide, who had received the ground as a gift from her husband, as a suburban villa on the Italian model. The house, which was built by the Italian architect

Opposite *Nymphenburg, the palace of the electors and kings of Bavaria.*

Below *The Amalienburg in the Park of Nymphenburg. The façade is broken by the curve of the central mirror salon.*

Agostino Barelli, forms only the central block of the present palace, the next Elector, Max Emanuel, had more ambitious plans than did his mother.

He was the friend and ally of Louis XIV of France and shared in the French defeat at Blenheim. He had to surrender his state to the Austrians, and lived for ten years in exile in Paris. But before his defeat he had already begun to develop Nymphenburg, the "Castle of the Nymphs" as his mother had named it, as a second Versailles. The architect, Enrico Zucalli, was under orders to preserve the palace of Henrietta, and in fact gave it the place of honor. Low two-story galleries link it with the buildings on the wings so that the original palace dominates the whole complex. Surprisingly, the Austrian occupying forces per-mitted building on the new palace to continue even during the elector's exile, but on his return to his capital of Munich with Joseph Effner, the architect who had designed his Paris house, the pace of the work on the grand electoral palace was increased.

The palace was extended further by Carl Albert, Max Emanuel's son and successor, who built the great crescent facing the palace to house government offices. In this way the Nymphenburg, its charming name a little out of place, came to embody the principles of absolutist rule that Louis XIV had tried to express in Versailles. The autocrat in his residence confronted the ministers and agents of his power. A further echo of Versailles is the canal that stretches towards the electoral capital of Munich.

The grand central hall of the main palace also dates from Max Emanuel, whose architects enlarged the windows of the façade to light it, but the hall's elegant rococo decoration by François Cuvilliés was added in the next reign. Cuvilliés' masterpiece, however, is the Amalienburg, one of the four pavilions in the grounds. Its elegant and original design centers on a circular saloon which breaks the main façade with a gently curving bay. Inside the walls are lined with mirrors framed in exquisite naturalistic stucco and wood designs that are answered by equally fine work on the ceiling. The color scheme of powder blue and silver contrasts with the yellows of the other rooms of the little palace. The other pavilions, all built for Max Emanuel, are the grotesque Magdalen Retreat, a kind of hermit's cave; the Badenburg or bath house; and the delightful little Pagodenburg.

Designed in the trend of the taste for *chinoiserie* by Joseph Effner, it is an unusual octagonally shaped building. The walls of the upper salon are lined with fine lacquer work panels and the room is furnished with pieces of *chinoiserie* by Parisian cabinet makers. Another fashion to leave its mark at Nymphenburg was the English garden, laid out in the early nineteenth century.

Blenheim Palace, one of the few English country mansions to bear that title, stands in the once royal park at Woodstock, in Oxfordshire; it is a monument to John Churchill, first Duke of Marlborough, one of the greatest soldiers England has produced. It is named after the great victory that he and Prince Eugene of Savoy won over the armies of France in 1704.

The Manor of Woodstock, given to Marlborough by Queen Anne, had been a favorite hunting lodge for English monarchs since the time of King Henry I, and when in the winter of 1704 Marlborough came with his architect Sir John Vanbrugh to survey the park, the sizeable medieval mansion begun by Henry II still stood. Here it was that Queen Elizabeth had been imprisoned while still a princess, by her sister Queen Mary. Vanbrugh hoped to incorporate the place into his designs, showing a somewhat avant-garde taste for the "Gothick". But the historic structure was destroyed in 1709 by order of Sarah, Duchess of Marlborough.

She it was who presided over the work at Blenheim, and she was soon bitterly at odds with the architect. Her main dispute was over the huge expense of his plans, for although Blenheim was a gift, Marlborough and his wife

Far left *The Mirror Room in the Amalienburg. This charming pavilion in the grounds of Nymphenburg Palace was the masterpiece of François Cuvilliés.*

Left *The formal gardens on the east and west terraces of Blenheim were restored in the twentieth century by the ninth duke. The water terrace seen here is in the grand tradition of formal baroque garden design.*

Below *The architect of Blenheim Palace, Sir John Vanbrugh, made his first reputation as a playwright. But although he was a gentleman and an amateur he designed some of the finest buildings in Europe. Blenheim was his masterpiece.*

The long Library at Blenheim, which was originally designed as a picture gallery.

fell from favor and the royal generosity dried up while there was still some of the building to be completed. Vanbrugh resigned from the commission in 1716 and the work continued under his brilliant assistant Nicholas Hawksmoor.

The visitor enters by the east court where the kitchens were housed and from here emerges into the great north court. The grouping of the windows, the way in which the architects have linked the wings and the central block by the subtle use of colonnades of pillars, and the dramatic impact of the great central porch are some of the features that lead historians of architecture to classify this court as one of the great achievements of the English baroque style. Over all there is the fantastic drama of the skyline in which statues and chimney stacks combine. The porch leads into the great entrance hall, its ceiling decorated by Sir James Thornhill and the walls embellished with trophies carved by Grinling Gibbons. Over the doorway are the arms of Queen Anne.

Beyond lies the salon from which, to the east, open out the Green Writing Room, the Red Drawing Room and the Green Drawing Room, and beyond them the private apartments. West of the salon are the three state rooms and the bedroom where the duke's most famous descendant, Sir Winston Churchill, was born on November 30 1874. Perhaps the finest room in the palace is the Long Library; according to tradition Lady Randolph Churchill, Sir Winston's Americanborn mother, was attending a ball here just before she had to leave the proceedings to give birth.

The park dates from 1760 when it was laid out by the famous gardener, Capability Brown. The meander of the little River Glyme broadens out and swells into a serpentine lake. The strangely truncated appearance of the bridge that crosses it derives from the fact that in Vanbrugh's scheme the bridge stood much higher but the lower courses were flooded by Brown's enlargement of the lake. It leads to the Elm Avenue that stretches away from the column of victory surmounted by a statue of Marlborough. The formal gardens of the original house were swept away in the quest for romantic naturalism that Brown and his school fostered. Thanks to the ninth duke, the formal terraces were restored to the west and east fronts, but the massive and elaborate parterre that originally stretched before the south front has gone for ever.

The palace at Versailles, painted by Pierre Patel the Elder in 1668, that is before the great wings and other additions undertaken by J. Hardouin-Mansart had been started.

THE great palace of the French Bourbon kings at **Versailles**, eleven miles to the south-west of Paris, was devoted to the glory of one man and of one idea. That man was King Louis XIV, who claimed the title of the Sun King; the idea was that of the French monarchy. Undoubtedly this is the most grandiose of European palaces and it was the subject of more jealous imitation than any other building in modern history. For Versailles seemed to epitomize all the pretensions of triumphant national monarchy, and by its scale and extravagance set a new standard for royal display, which was to be frequently imitated.

The entrance to the palace of Versailles is approached through the great Cour d'Honneur *flanked by wings of the palace.*

The original château had been built in the 1620s and 1630s for King Louis XIII. It was quite subsidiary in importance to St Germain or Fontainebleau, it was domestically decorated and was charmingly nick-named the "house of cards". While it might offer good hunting and a pleasant retreat from the cares of state, the site had nothing to recommend it as a permanent residence. Saint-Simon, a mordant critic of Louis XIV's court, said of Versailles that it was "the saddest of places, without a view, without woods and without water". Others were to call it the "favorite without merit". The terrain was a mixture of unstable sandy soils and marshlands and the air was notoriously unhealthy. Thousands of workmen died of marsh fever while the work was in progress and the bodies of the dead were taken by the cartload for burial at night, so as not to scare off new recruits.

Jean Baptiste Colbert, the king's great minister, protested against the extravagance, but Louis was inflexible. He conceived the idea of this greatest of all palaces after a visit to Vaux le Vicomte, built by Nicholas Fouquet, the superintendent of finances, at the beginning of his reign. Soon after the young king's visit in 1661 the minister was disgraced and the talented group of architects and designers who had worked for him entered the royal service. Among them were the architect Louis le Vau, the painter Charles le Brun and the landscape gardener, André le Nôtre.

At Versailles the king ordered Le Vau to preserve the palace built by his father. This was done by enclosing the U-shaped building with two wings and an open terrace along the garden façade on the base of the U. The inside

façades can be seen today enclosing the Marble Court. After Le Vau's death the works at Versailles were continued by Jules Hardouin, the nephew of the famous architect François Mansart whose surname he adopted. Hardouin-Mansart designed the final massive group of buildings that we see today. He flanked Le Vau's central block with two huge wings to give the garden façade a total length of a quarter of a mile. Like Le Vau he used the low-pitched roofs characteristic of Italy rather than the steep roofs of earlier French styles. This low skyline, combined with the immense length of the buildings and the sober, repeating classical details of the windows, create what has been called the "regal monotony of the Park Front of Versailles".

The architect achieved a far more exciting conception in the Orangery where the dignified simplicity of the Doric columns on the façade is emphasized and enhanced within by the quiet strength of the simple barrel-vaulting. But Hardouin-Mansart's most sensational work is the Hall of Mirrors, which he built in the recessed terrace that Le Vau had left on the garden façade. It is a huge gallery lined with mirrors on the wall facing the windows and richly decorated with paintings supervised by Charles le Brun. It was to be copied more than any other feature of the palace.

Throughout Versailles the decorations and furnishings were of the same extravagant and heavy splendor; they were supplied by the Royal Furniture Factory at Gobelins. This was set up by Colbert and the king, partly as an act of artistic patronage and partly to save foreign exchange on the import of luxury goods. The factory was directed by Le Brun

The Hall of Mirrors at Versailles, one of the most imitated rooms in the history of architecture. Here William I of Prussia was proclaimed Emperor of Germany in 1870; here the chief of the treaties ending the First World War was signed in 1919.

who provided designs for tapestries and furnishings of all types. Thanks to the demand of Versailles Gobelins was the factory of a new style in French design—the style Louis Quatorze. Presided over by such a monarch and such a minister, both brilliant as administrators though deficient in inspiration, the style could not help but be immensely lavish, professional and often pompous. The true genius of French art descends through such masters as La Tour, Poussin, Claude, Watteau and Chardin. Coypel the painter and Coysevox the sculptor, whose works proliferate with that of Le Brun at Versailles are, like him, comparatively minor, though prolific, artists.

In palace and grounds the theme of the Sun King is repeated in statuary and paint. The Grand Apartments of the king survive in their original decorations. It was here that he lived his unbelievably public life. The palace was thronged daily with courtiers, workmen, servants and visitors from every walk of life. Virtually anyone was entitled to have access to the king's presence so long as he wore a sword, the badge of a gentleman's rank. Swords could be hired for a modest charge at the gate. The morning levée (reception), when the king rose from his bed, his meals and his retiring to bed at night were all fully public

functions watched by scores of people. In 1687 the Grand Trianon was built in the grounds on the site of the demolished village of Trianon. It was a mere mansion designed to give Louis more privacy than he could enjoy at the great palace.

The tourists could not pass through the grand palace without seeing on every side artistic propaganda of the king's greatness. Of the statues in the main courtyard, that of Louis was the largest. In the War Drawing Room the trophies of victory were dominated by an oval relief showing the mounted monarch in triumph; the Mars Room was covered with depictions of his heroic actions. Equally evident, at least to the nostrils, must have been the appalling sanitation. The vast buildings housed hundreds of permanent and semi-permanent residents from members of the royal family and courtiers, to officials and state guests. Courtiers did not hesitate to use the grand staircases as latrines when in emergency, while the ornamental pools in the Grand Parterre d'Eau, the Great Water Garden, regularly had to be cleared of filth and rubbish.

The grounds beyond the formal gardens were on a scale to match the palace. To force the unpromising terrain to fit Le Nôtre's grand concept required vast excavations and major

Opposite *The Temple of Love in the grounds of Versailles.*

Below *The* Cour d'Honneur *at Fontainebleau dates mostly from the sixteenth century. The grand staircase was added in the seventeenth century.*

hydraulic works which cost thousands of lives and millions of *livres*. A waterworks was built on the Seine at Marly which in its day was considered one of the wonders of the world. It continued in use until 1804 but soon after its completion the water intended for Versailles had to be diverted to yet another royal palace that Louis commanded, at Marly itself. After twenty years, the attempt to bring water from the river Eure had to be abandoned, and instead channels, pipes, vaults and aqueducts were constructed, in all some ninety-eight miles in length, to collect the waters of the plain between Versailles and Rambouillet. Yet the water supply was still not sufficient and the fountains of the Grand Parterre d'Eau were only played to their full extent when the king himself was walking in the grounds. The elegant terraces and graveled walks led the visitor to the main grounds beyond, dominated by the grand avenue of trees with smaller walks branching off to secluded bowers and alcoves decorated with urns and statuary. In the distance, along the main axis of the palace, stretched the Grand Canal, 200 feet wide and a mile long. In its heyday it was covered by pleasure craft of all sorts, among them a replica of a galley, a brigantine and a Venetian gondola with real Venetian gondoliers.

After Louis's death, Versailles fell from favor for a time, but his successor Louis XV did return there in the 1740s. The sumptuous opera house was one of the chief additions made by his court architect, Ange-Jacques Gabriel; the other was the charming house, the Petit Trianon. This became the favorite haunt of Louis XVI's queen, Marie Antoinette. Here she and her ladies cultivated a pastoral idyll, pretending to be shepherdesses and dairymaids, enjoying the comforts of the rich while aping the simplicity of the poor.

After the first years of the Revolution, during which Versailles was well looked after, looters and speculators plundered its treasures and the buildings decayed. Not until the twentieth century was this vast showpiece palace properly restored. Furniture and furnishings that had been scattered through the museums of France were brought back and the gardens were restored to something near their first conception.

Long before the building of Versailles, the French kings had had their country residence at **Fontainebleau**, some forty miles to the south of Paris. The name is a corruption of the medieval Latin, Fons Bliaudi, or the "fountain of Bliaud". In the twelfth century King Louis VII built a chapel here, and his grandson,

St Louis IX (d. 1270), built the large tower that still forms the focus of the Oval Courtyard. Other parts of the medieval palace fell into ruin during the fifteenth century, but in 1528 King Francis I began the building of a grand new royal residence.

Like his great rival Henry VIII of England, Francis I was a lavish builder, but unlike most of Henry's buildings, which have disappeared, Fontainebleau remains as a monument in the history of French art. The royal patron was inspired by the scholarship and art of the Italian Renaissance, and his architect, Giles le Breton, introduced the Italian idiom into his basically French style. He designed the Golden Gate, the Gallery of Francis I and the Cour du Cheval Blanc (the White Horse Courtyard), which is now the main entrance to the palace. The flamboyant staircase, badly out of scale with the rest of the façade, is the work of the seventeenth-century architect Philibert Delorme. Other additions were made in the eighteenth century, among them the decorations to the Salle du Conseil by François Boucher and the Great Pavilion built by the architect Ange-Jacques Gabriel for King Louis XV. Napoleon, who called Fontainebleau "the house of centuries, the seat of kings", lived here in preference to Versailles. In 1804 the architects Percier and Fontaine were moved from work at Malmaison to supervise the renovation of the palace, while an army of craftsmen and designers were put to work preparing furniture and decoration in the new Empire style.

However, nothing of the later ages can compete with the achievements of the reign of Francis I. Chief among these is the Gallery of Francis I, completed in 1531. The decorations were supervised by the Florentine painter Il Rosso and took ten years to complete. Deep wainscotting of carved walnut paneling runs

Below The magnificent Galerie François Ier, one of the finest schemes of interior decoration in Europe, was completed in 1531.

Bottom The façade and gardens at Schönbrunn, Vienna, the palace of Empress Maria Theresa.

the length of the walls, while above it is one of the finest and most coherent schemes of painted panels and stucco to be found in Europe. The thirteen paintings deal with allegorical subjects beloved of Renaissance scholarship, the chief one being the battle of the Lapiths and Centaurs, the symbol of the battle between culture and barbarism. Il Rosso's work was succeeded in 1541 by Primaticcio, who even eclipsed the fame of his master with his work in the Gallery of Ulysses. This was studied by artists from all over Europe until, two centuries later, it was destroyed and replaced by the Great Pavilion of Louis XV. Yet the school of artists led by Il Rosso and Primaticcio had a seminal influence in French art.

Throughout its history the French Bourbon dynasty was in conflict with the House of Habsburg, which long ruled Spain and the Austrian Empire. The seat of the Austrian Habsburgs was the **Palace of Schönbrunn** at

Below *The Great Gallery at Schönbrunn. The mirrors facing the windows show the influence of the Hall of Mirrors at Versailles.*

Bottom *The garden façade of Schönbrunn viewed from a fountain in the gardens down one of the carefully contrived vistas.*

Vienna. There had been a hunting lodge on the site since the fourteenth century, but in 1569 the Emperor Maximilian II rebuilt it on a grander scale. Maximilian's work was devastated by a Hungarian incursion in 1605, but the Emperor Matthias erected a new palace, and while the work was in progress the little spring, the "beautiful spring" that gave the palace its name, was discovered in the grounds. In the 1680s, the Turkish armies besieging Vienna destroyed the palace of Matthias, and the building that we know today was built from 1696 to 1713 on the design of J. B. Fischer von Erlach, with certain additions during the eighteenth century. Von Erlach's baroque style was shaped by his training in Rome and by French styles. Schönbrunn was to emulate Versailles, and Fischer's first plans were on a more impressive scale than even his French model; they had to be abandoned for reasons of cost. Life at Schönbrunn reached its zenith in the reign of the Empress Maria Theresa. The triumphal gate known as the Gloriette was erected to celebrate her victory over Prussia at the battle of Kolin in 1757. From 1805 to 1809, the palace was the headquarters of the victorious Napoleon; it was here that his son by the Austrian princess Marie Louise lived after his father's final defeat in 1815. From 1848 to 1916 Schönbrunn was the residence of the Emperor Francis Joseph I.

The main palace is grouped around a great courtyard with one long wing running away to the left of the entrance gateway and a smaller wing to the right. Here was the imperial coach house, which is now among the world's finest coaching museums and including in its treasures the imperial coronation coach built about the year 1700. The lavish scale of the interiors reflects Austria's past greatness, but the lasting impression is one of elegance. The taste for *chinoiserie* is much in evidence. The Blue Salon is papered in hand-painted Chinese wallpaper. Another room, which Napoleon used as his study, is paneled in fine lacquer work, while the walls of a third are lined in blue and white porcelain. The remarkable Salon of the Million, so-called because of the cost of its decoration, has a fine wainscotting in Chinese rosewood which is set with priceless Persian and Mogul miniatures brought back from Istanbul by one of Maria Theresa's ambassadors. In 1762, the Hall of Mirrors served as the concert hall for a programme given by the brilliant young Mozart, then aged six, with his nine-year-old sister.

The gardens are laid out in the formal French style, but the shaded tree walks and the glistening white statuary create an intimate atmosphere, and off one of the main avenues is the fountain through which the "beautiful spring" of Schönbrunn plays.

"You will be better lodged than I am at the Tuileries." This was Napoleon's comment on the **Royal Palace Madrid** to his brother Joseph whom he had installed as King of Spain. It stands on a height that falls away sharply to west and north; behind are the royal gardens laid out first in the sixteenth century on a site still known as the Campo del Moro. The palace was begun in 1738 for the Bourbon King Philip V, who first hired the architect Felipe Juvara. Although Philip was delighted by the lavish scheme that Juvara proposed, he reluctantly had to abandon the project as too expensive. The visitor to the luxurious apartments of the Royal Palace today may be forgiven for wondering what kind of a scheme it was that was to be more expensive than this. In fact the king was still too ambitious. He had intended to crown the roof with a series of colossal statues of the kings of Spain, but they were found to be too heavy for the structure and were removed to the grounds.

Instead of Juvara, G. B. Sacchetti of Turin was chosen to design the palace, and work began on the actual construction in 1738. The scale and splendor of the interior is proclaimed by the magnificent main staircase; lofty and austere, the columns support a handsome vaulted ceiling and the whole composition comes alive under the light streaming through the circular windows above the colonnade. Two regal lions crouch on the balustrade at the head of the first flight as though guarding the stairway to the main apartments above. Lions also stand guard in the throne room, four superb and ferocious sculptures flanking the steps that lead up to the throne dais. The treasures of the palace include the marvelous Sala del Gasparini with its gilded stucco work; the exquisite porcelain salon, one of the finest of its type in Europe with its walls lined from floor to ceiling in delicate porcelain, and the Armeria Real. Housed in the west wing this is one of the richest collections of armor in the world.

Like most of Europe's royal palaces, that at Madrid is now open to tourists. If the plans to restore the monarchy after Franco's death are realized it may have the rare distinction of a royal residence returned to royal use in the second half of the twentieth century.

The Sala del Gasparini in the Royal Palace,
Madrid. The great palaces of the past were lit by
thousands of candles, and the chandeliers that
held them were brilliant achievements of the
glassmaker's art.

Below *The* porte-cochère *on the north entrance front of the White House, reaching as it does from ground to roof level, is an unusual and* imaginative feature. The columns are in the Ionic style of ancient Greek architecture.

Our last great building that is a seat of authority is strictly speaking no palace at all, though its scale and elegance entitle it to be described in company with the other official residences of the heads of state of great powers. It stands on the south side of Pennsylvania Avenue, in Washington, DC, and it is the office and residence of the President of the United States of America. The **White House** has actually been white ever since 1814. In that year British troops set fire to the fabric and gutted the building, and after the conclusion of hostilities it was given a coat of white paint. But it had been popularly known as the White House even before that time although the name was not officially adopted until the presidency of Theodore Roosevelt (1901–09), when it was engraved on the presidential stationery. The architect of the original "palace" (it was in fact so designated

Above *In 1948 work was finished on a semicircular colonnaded balcony on the south front of the White House; it balances the effect of the* porte-corchère *over the main entrance at the front of the building.*

on the plans) was the Irish-born James Hoban, who had come to the States in 1789 in his late twenties, and who won the commission by public competition three years later. The site had been chosen by President George Washington, and Hoban's bold and stately design is admirably adapted to the setting and the ideals of the founding fathers of the Republic. The main building is 170 feet long and 85 feet wide; the east and west terraces, the executive office and the east wing are among the later additions. Within there are spacious and elegantly proportioned rooms, among them the East Room, where large state receptions are usually held. The Red Room and the Green Room are used for more intimate occasions or private parties restricted to the president's personal guests. Probably the most famous part of the White House is the elliptical Blue Room, which was used by President John Kennedy for social and diplomatic receptions, and is one of the handsomest apartments.

Despite Washington's close involvement with the planning of the White House, he did not live there. The work was only completed in 1799 and the first president to take up official residence was John Adams in 1800. Like Whitehall in London, the White House has given its name to the administration based on it. It is the oldest public building in Washington and one of the finest.

The land of the Tsars

THE **Kremlin** stands on the left bank of the Moskva River on a range of low hills. In the Russian the word *kreml* means high town or citadel: the Kremlin is a cluster of palaces and cathedrals like a little town within the city of Moscow. The first fortress on the site, a comparatively humble wood rampart, was built in the twelfth century at a time when Russia was hardly a name. In the following century the numerous Russian states were overrun by the Mongols under the successors of Genghis Khan, and for nearly two centuries their rulers competed against one another for the favor of the Mongol Khans and the leadership of "all the Russias". In the 1360s Dmitri Donskoi, Grand Duke of Moscow and one of the first to defy the power of the Mongols, rebuilt the Kremlin to enclose a very much larger area. The city was soon to be sacked in

Mongol reprisals, but the citadel stood firm. A hundred years after Donskoi's death the rulers of Moscow had succeeded in wresting the leadership of the Russian states from the Khanate.

In 1485, Grand Duke Ivan III of Moscow launched a massive building program on the Kremlin hill. New palaces and churches began to rise and the white stone walls of Dmitri Donskoi were replaced by the brick ones that still stand today. These enclose a triangular area of some seventy acres and are more than a mile in circumference. Originally they were protected by water, for the Kremlin is at the confluence of the little Neglinnaya River, now covered over, and the Moskva. A moat joining the two rivers completed the encirclement; it ran along the wall that borders Red Square and has long since been filled in. The walls are guarded by twenty towers and are pierced by numerous gates. In 1935 five of these towers were adorned with great red stars. From 6 to 12 feet high and made of rubies from the Ural mines, they are illuminated every night as the visual emblem that the Kremlin, once the fortress of the tsars, is now a communist citadel.

Ivan III chose Italian architects, for the fame of the Renaissance had reached even distant Russia. Pietro Solario and Marco Ruffo, called "the Franks" by the Russians, built the Kremlin walls on the model of the Sforza Palace at Milan. During these years, 1485 to 1508, Russian architects from Pskov were directing the work on the great Cathedral of the Annunciation, with its three apses and three altars. Their orders were to copy the Cathedral of Vladimir which had been the capital of the Grand Duchy before the rise of Moscow. The cathedral's iconostasis, a screen carrying sacred icons, divides the altars and the bishop's throne from the main church. Among the icons that it carries are those attributed to Theophanes the Greek and the great early fifteenth century painter, Andrei Rublev, whose work has achieved world-wide fame.

The Cathedral of the Assumption, or the Dormition, largest of the Kremlin churches, was also intended as a copy of a church at Vladimir. But here the architect was another Italian, Rodolfo Fioravanti, and he only copied the central part with its five cupolas, arcades and portals. In fact his design, which included a terrace of twin arcades, caused something of a sensation when it was built. The cathedral was the burial place of the Patriarchs and Metropolitans of the Russian

Orthodox Church and was also the coronation church of the tsars. The frescoes on the walls were renewed for each coronation so that the masterpieces of earlier ages were obliterated by later work. The tsars themselves were buried in the Cathedral of the Archangel Michael, completed in 1509. It is here that the founder of the modern Kremlin, Grand Duke Ivan, is buried. Again the architect was Italian, Alevisio Novi of Milan, and again there is a dramatic façade with huge shells in place of the traditional arcades at first story level. The portals are embellished with a wealth of carvings.

At this time too, a church was built to St John the Baptist, but this was demolished in the nineteenth century because Tsar Nicholas I found it obscured the view from his new palace of the new Cathedral of the Saviour. The Great Kremlin Palace, designed by a German architect, was built on the site of an earlier one built for the Empress Elizabeth by the Italian Rastrelli. Its state rooms, which include the hall of St George, 200 feet long and the largest room in the Kremlin, are used for official state receptions, while the palace itself is the seat of the Supreme Soviet of the USSR and also of the Soviet of the Russian Socialist Republic. The vast hall of the Supreme Soviet is the result of combining the St Andrew and St Alexander rooms of the former palace.

Nicholas I's Great Palace effectively obscures the splendid façade of the baroque Terems Palace; nearby is the Facets Palace built by Ruffo and Solario in the 1490s. In the throne room here, the tsars received the homage of their chief nobles during the coronation ceremony, and the walls depict the supposed transmission of the insignia of the Byzantine empire to Duke Vladimir Monomakh.

The Senate House, built in the 1770s and 1780s for a national assembly called by Catherine the Great but never held, is the official headquarters of the Soviet Government. Here Lenin's room, on the top floor of the east wing, is preserved as it was on the day he died. The most recent building on this site is the Congress Building inaugurated in 1961; its vast Conference Hall seats no fewer than 6,000. It is a huge building, but the architects were given a strict height limit so that the skyline of the historic Kremlin should not be broken; as a result many of the facilities are in the extensive basements. It is the latest addition to an historic and much built-over site and it emphasizes the dual character of the Kremlin as a home of government as well as a centre of fine architecture and cultural treasures.

In the early eighteenth century Moscow lost its primacy as a national capital to the new city of Leningrad. One of the finest cities in Europe, it was founded by Tsar Peter the Great as a new capital of a state that he was determined to modernize from top to bottom. The change of capital was intended to symbolize the new Russia, and its site, with access to the Baltic Sea, emphasized the outward

Far left *The towers and spires of the Kremlin by night.*

Left *The Kremlin, from across the Moskva River. In the center of the picture is the late eighteenth-century Senate House.*

Bottom left and below *The gold leaf of the cathedrals in the Kremlin is kept in constant repair at public expense even under the Communist regime. These architectural masterpieces are considered part of the national heritage.*

looking nature of the new regime. Work was begun in 1703 on the banks of the Neva River where it flows into the Gulf of Finland, an arm of the Baltic. It was virgin land, and as a site was marshy and not well suited for heavy building works. Yet the superb city went ahead at great speed and is a monument to eighteenth-century town planning.

The first palace was completed in 1711 and ten years later another was built next to it, but both these were demolished for the **Winter Palace**, commissioned by the Empress Elizabeth from her court architect Bartolommeo Francesco Rastrelli, who designed many of the public buildings in Leningrad. The palace stands on the banks of the Neva River and presents a breath-taking spectacle of blue and white from across the water.

From its completion in 1764 until 1917 it was the chief palace of the tsars. It fell to the revolutionaries of October 1917 when shots fired on it from the cruiser *Aurora* were the signal for the beginning of armed insurrections against the provisional post-tsarist government of Kerensky, based in the palace.

A fire in 1837 destroyed much of the interior décor, though an example of Rastrelli's work here survives over the Jordan Doorway in the river façade. It was from this doorway that the tsars left the palace for a ceremonial baptism at the church festival of the Epiphany. A magnificent staircase of white Carrara marble sweeps down to the door from the tsar's private apartments. Adjoining the palace is the Hermitage. The original building was erected by the Empress Catherine the Great to house her collection of art, and today the Hermitage is one of the very greatest of the world's museums. In addition to 8000 paintings by every European master of importance, from Rembrandt to Picasso, there are rich archaeological collections from all over the world. Outstanding among them are the fabulous gold treasures of the ancient Scythians, whose culture once flourished in central Russia.

A few miles south of Leningrad lies the town which is now known as Pushkin, from its associations with the great Russian writer. Until the Revolution, however, it was known as **Tsarskoye Selo**, the "Tsar's Village",

because here and at the neighboring town of Pavlovsk were the summer palaces of Catherine the Great and her successors, palaces on a scale which rivaled those in the capitals of Moscow and Leningrad. The townships became the focus of high society during the summer months. The railway from St Petersburg to Tsarskoye Selo, built in 1837, was the first in Russia, and in the 1840s it was used by hundreds of pleasure seekers coming out to the dances and balls presided over by the fabulous Johann Strauss, the Waltz King. The electric lighting system installed in these smart suburbs and the royal palaces there was the first in commercial service anywhere in the world. After the Revolution the pleasure ground of the aristocracy was turned over to the children for parks and recreation grounds, and for a time the little town was known as Dietskoye Selo or "Children's Village".

The magnificent façade stretches for 950 feet, and its fresh blue and white decoration, picked out in gold, seems to cast a wistful eye back to the age of imperial elegance. Yet what the modern tourist sees is, surprisingly, the fruit

Opposite *The Winter Palace as we see it today is the result of patient restoration work since the Second World War.*

Top *The Malachite Room in the Winter Palace. Throughout the palace the magnificent floors were lovingly brought back to their original beauty after the damage of the war.*

Above *An eighteenth-century engraving of the Winter Palace in Leningrad with the vast Admiralty Square in front of it.*

Below *The Rastrelli Pavilion in the grounds of the Summer Palace built by the Italian architect for the Russian Empress Catherine the Great.*

Bottom *The garden front of the Summer Palace at Tsarskoye Selo, which has recently been restored to its original splendor.*

of restoration work of the last two decades. In fact all the monuments of Russia's past, except some of the churches, are in this magnificent state of preservation. The domes of the Kremlin are regularly re-gilded with gold leaf, and millions of roubles have been spent since the war on painstaking reconstructions of palaces damaged during the terrible bombardments of the Second World War. The western mind might construe this as sound investment in tourism, but the restoration was going on long before Russia was opened up to tourism in the way it is now. For the average Russian money spent like this is a tribute of respect to their ancestors. For if it was the aristocrats who sponsored the building of these massive and luxurious homes for their own comfort, it was the labor of thousands of oppressed serfs which brought them to completion. The Russian of today is proud to be descended from this peasant stock and is proud of the work that it achieved.

*The great front staircase in the Summer Palace at
Tsarskoye Selo.*

The Summer Palace of Catherine the Great at Tsarskoye Selo was systematically gutted by the German army before it retreated in 1942. The

interiors had to be completely rebuilt by modern craftsmen.

There are few places where the work of restoration has been more laborious and complete than the Catherine Palace at Tsarskoye Selo, which indeed is still in progress. For this magnificent monument was occupied by the German armies that besieged Leningrad for almost two years between 1941 and 1943. Much of the city was laid in ruins by the bombardment, but the Summer Palace was systematically gutted before the Germans finally withdrew. The interior of the palace as it appears today is almost entirely the work of modern craftsmen. One room, however, not even they could replace. This is the famed Amber Room, once called the eighth wonder of the world and removed along with countless other treasures before the demolition squads moved in. The paneling consisted of exquisite carving in amber, and miniatures with figures so tiny that they could only be properly seen with the aid of a magnifying glass. The work was done for the Prussian King Frederick I by a German architect and jeweler but came to Russia when King Frederick William presented it to Peter the Great as a gift. Such a present was kingly indeed and when the room was moved to the Summer Palace at the behest of the Empress Elizabeth the new setting required adjustments to the layout of the panels which enabled the Russian court jeweler to enhance this magical work of art still further.

When the war ended in 1945 Russia had more pressing matters to consider than the recovery of art treasures looted by the invaders. But as early as 1949 a commission was set up to track down and claim such plunder, and at the head of its list was the Amber Room from Tsarskoye Selo.

Under the sign of the crescent

A colonnade in the Alhambra palace, Granada. The fine stalactite molding over the arches is characteristic of this great Moorish palace.

AL-QAL' AL-HAMRA, the Red Fortress, still dominates the town of Granada as a reminder of the 750 years of Islamic rule in southern Spain. It presents a formidable exterior to the visitor, but inside the walls he discovers a beautiful palace. The site, originally an arid outcrop of red sandstone, had been fortified since the ninth century, but the **Alhambra** we see today was built in the mid-thirteenth century by Mohammed I of Granada. With the capture of the great Islamic city of Cordoba in 1236, the Christian kings of Spain had scored a massive success, and the kingdom of Granada to the south appeared to be the next candidate for conquest.

Mohammed's first concern was to strengthen his defenses, and according to legend he built the fortress of Alcazaba protected by the three great towers known as the Watch Tower, the Homage Tower and the Quebrada Tower. Yusuf I (1333–54) completed the fortifications with the elaborate entrance known as the Puerta de las Armas. The palace enclosure stretches for some 300 yards eastward from the Alcazaba. It is surrounded by a strong wall guarded by towers at regular intervals and entered by the Puerto de Hierro on the north wall and the magnificent Puerta de la Justitia on the south. Like the Puerta de las Armas, both these have entrance passages designed so as to force an attacker to double back on his tracks and run the gauntlet of concealed fire from the defense. The Gate of Justice, to give it its English title, is now the main entrance to the Alhambra. It too was built by Yusuf and it was the site of the ruler's open-air court. The open hand carved in the keystone of the arch is a religious emblem of Islam.

The Alhambra fell to the Catholic kings in 1492. The conquest marked the end of the Muslim rule in Spain and must have seemed a great deal more important than the fact that one of Queen Isabella's sea captains, a certain Cristoforo Colombo from Genoa, had claimed to discover a westward passage to the Indies. After the Conquest some of the buildings within the precincts were destroyed and the rest of the palace was left to fall into decay until restoration work began in the 1820s.

The contrast between the fortress area and the palace is vivid. After the stern walls of the Alcazaba, the courtyards and colonnades, lush well-kept gardens and lofty audience chambers, seem like some magical stage set for the Arabian Nights. Fountains and ornamental pools are everywhere so that the place seems alive with the sight and sound of water; reflections dapple on the walls and pillars, while the gentle play of fountains is heard in every court. The conversion of the parched rocky site is due to the aqueduct built by Mohammed I, big enough to supply the military garrison and the gardens that were yet to be laid out.

The Court of Myrtles, one of the most beautiful, was built by Mohammed V (1362–91). At the center of the court is an ornamental pool fringed with myrtle trees, while at either end a porchway flanked by six colonnaded arches gives access to the court from other parts of the palace. On the north side an ante-room led to the Hall of the Ambassadors. This is the literal English equivalent of the Spanish *comares,* but it seems likely that this word itself came from a misunderstanding of the Arabic *qamariyya,* a style of colored glass developed in Cairo in the thirteenth century. The now empty windows of the hall were once probably glazed with vibrant stained glass; the hall, which may have been the throne room, is one of the triumphs of Muslim architecture in Spain.

The most famous part of the whole palace is the Court of the Lions. At its center is the exquisite fountain that gives the court its name. It consists of an alabaster basin rising from a platform borne up on the backs of twelve marble lions. They are carved in coarse brutal lines that contrast effectively with the delicacy of the rest of the court. This is more than a hundred feet long and sixty wide, and is decorated with close-set slender colonnades and rills of water running in channels let into the floor. Beyond are the beautiful Generalife Gardens, a courtyard set with ornamental

Top *The Court of Myrtles in the Alhambra is a magical combination of water, trees and stone, characteristic of Moorish architecture.*

Above *The elegant fountains and luxuriant vegetation in the Generalife Gardens of the Alhambra make it hard to realize that the palace was built on an arid outcrop of red and sunbaked rock.*

Opposite *Looking into the Court of Lions at the Alhambra.*

Below *The stylised forms of the lions supporting the fountain make an almost brutal contrast with delicately carved arcades.*

Opposite *The Audience Pavilion of the sultans in the Topkapi palace.*

trees and shrubs and flowers, divided by a long narrow pool or canal with fountains playing into it from either side.

The royal apartments include the Hall of Kings and the Room of the Two Sisters. The latter is called after two marble slabs that form part of the pavement, and the room, like that of the "Abencerrajes" on the opposite side of the Court of Lions, has a magnificent ceiling of "honeycomb" or stalactite vaulting. These ceilings are made up of more than 5000 facets of polished stone and seem to float on the sunbeams that slant into the room through the windows below them. Throughout the Alhambra is a poem of light, trees and water. It remains one of the most beautiful palaces in the world, and there can be no doubt that before its conquest in 1492, it was the most civilized and elegant royal residence in Europe.

In the middle of the fifteenth century a new Islamic power established itself on the Mediterranean with the conquest of Constantinople in 1453 by the Turkish sultan, Mehmet II. From then until the mid-nineteenth century the **Topkapi Palace** was the chief residence of the Sultans. It is built on an ancient site which was first the acropolis of a classical Greek city. Then in 313 the Roman emperor Constantine founded his new eastern capital there, called Constantinople after him – the Turkish version of the name is Istanbul. The site commands a fine position overlooking the Bosphorus, the Golden Horn and the Sea of Marmora.

Sultan Mehmet II's first palace was the Old Seraglio on a site now occupied by Istanbul University but he transferred his government to Yeni Sarayi, the "New Palace", as soon as its walls were completed in the

1470s. The name was changed to Topkapi Sarayi, Cannon Gate Palace, in the eighteenth century when the Sultan Ahmet III built a palace whose entrance was guarded by two cannons. The entrance was destroyed by fire in 1863, but the name has stuck.

Topkapi takes the form of a number of courtyards, one behind the other. The largest is the Second or Public Courtyard. Down one side are the kitchens, remarkable even for a palace. They formerly employed more than 1000 chefs, pastry cooks and scullions, and prepared regular daily menus for 5000 people; for a banquet the guest list could number as many as 10,000. Today the kitchen buildings house one of the most extensive and breath-taking collections of porcelain in the world. It includes complete dinner services of thousands of pieces from the Sung to Ming dynasties (960–1343), some presented to the

sultans by the Chinese emperors, other made to special order.

From the public courtyard, privileged visitors passed through the Bab i Saadet, the Gate of Happiness, guarded by White Eunuchs of the sultan's personal bodyguard, to the sultan's state quarters. Immediately behind the gate is the beautiful pavilion which was the audience chamber where the sultan received foreign ambassadors. Behind that is the white marble library of Sultan Ahmet III, which holds some 6000 unpublished Greek and Arabic manuscripts. In the buildings that line the south-east side of the third court is a fine exhibition of miniature portraits and superbly illuminated Korans, some the work of the sultans themselves. Next comes the treasure house containing the personal possessions of the sultans; among these perhaps the most remarkable is a little chess set. It

Sultan Selim giving an audience in a courtyard of the Topkapi palace.

consists of thirty-two cylinders of solid flawless rock crystal, of various heights to indicate the different pieces. The opposing sides are distinguished quite easily–one has an emerald set in gold on the top of each cylinder, the other has a ruby. This abstract design, combining simplicity with luxury, makes an unforgettable impression amidst the technicolor opulence of the Topkapi Palace.

Another room holds the thrones, among them the throne of the Persian Shah Ismail, captured by Sultan Selim I in his wars against Persia. The throne is in the form of a low wide platform with a low curved back; it is decorated with red and green enamels set in gold and is encrusted with some 25,000 jewels. In the fourth room of the treasury can be seen the imperial jewel collection; it includes a diamond of 86 carats and a single uncut emerald mined intact and weighing 3260 kg.

But for the faithful of the Muslim world all these riches pale before the relics of the Prophet, among them two ceremonial swords in gold and precious stones and, the most sacred of all, the cloak of Mohammed.

A door off the third courtyard leads to the Harem, the quarters of the sultans' wives and concubines, a subject of perennial fascination to the western mind. It is a warren of rooms, and in the high days of the sultanate was a a hive of plotting and political intrigue as the ladies of the court maneuvered for position on behalf of themselves and their sons.

Dolmabahce, literally the "filled-in garden", was constructed along the coast of the Bosphorus for Sultan Ahmet I (1603–17). An unattractive low-lying and marshy site was converted into beautiful gardens where a wooden pavilion or "kiosk" provided the sultan with a charming summer residence just outside his capital of Istanbul. In the early

Below *Looking over the roofs of the Topkapi palace to the blue waters of the Bosphorus.*

Bottom *The first palace of Dolmabahce was built on the shores of the Bosphorus as a summer residence for the sultans in the seventeenth century. The present buildings date from the 1840s.*

nineteenth century the wooden buildings were destroyed by fire and then, in 1853, a splendid new stone palace began to rise on the site at the orders of Sultan Abdulmecit.

Within the high stone walls and wrought iron railings bounding the sea coast are a number of two-storied buildings in glistening white marble. At the center stands the tallest of them, housing the throne room. The others provided the sultan's private apartments; those for his mother; the accommodation for the ladies of the harem; and a special suite for the heir to the throne. The new palace was far bigger than its predecessors, but the plan, with its numerous separate residences, was in the Turkish tradition of pleasure gardens and courtyards dotted with kiosks.

Nevertheless, the style of the architecture shows that the Turkish architect Baliyan looked to Europe for his models. The influence of Versailles is apparent even here,

Below *The interiors of Dolmabahce are a fascinating blend of oriental and nineteenth-century European domestic decoration.*

Bottom *The main entrance gate to Dolmabahce Palace shows a remarkable admixture of classical, baroque and oriental styles.*

though Dolmabahce achieves a unique effect from the way in which the European baroque has been blended with Eastern and Indian motifs. The brilliant white of the marble façades under the Mediterranean sun, the handsome water frontage with its graceful and lofty wrought-iron palings and the dark but vibrant blue-greens of the cypress trees in the gardens combine to magical effect. Within, the European influence becomes much more apparent. The furniture and décor, much of it by French and Italian craftsmen, the fine English long-case clocks and many other features give the flavor of a nineteenth-century European bourgeois interior, while the lavish use of porphyry and crystal throughout emphasize the oriental opulence of the setting.

After the overthrow of Sultan Abdul Aziz in 1876 and the establishment of a more liberal regime, Dolmabahce was used for the first session of the Turkish house of Representatives in March 1877. Since 1923, when the great Kemal Ataturk proclaimed the founding of the Turkish Republic, it has been the Presidential Palace. Ataturk, the first president, died here, in room 71, on November 10, 1938.

The library in Napoleon's charming domestic palace at Malmaison.

*In this early nineteenth-century watercolor by
Lefebvre-Marchand, the charmingly domestic air
of Malmaison is very apparent.*

MOST of the buildings in this book are
grand, not to say grandiose, expressions
of wealth and power. In this chapter we take a
look at a group of residences which, either by
intention or by chance, have a somewhat
more domestic atmosphere. Hampton Court,
for example, was rebuilt at the end of the
seventeenth century with the intention of
outshining even Versailles. But the style of the
building, coupled with a shortage of funds,
resulted in a palace, which despite these
ambitious plans is clearly designed to be lived
in. **Malmaison,** on the other hand, was
intentionally kept on a modest scale even when
it became the residence of Napoleon Bonaparte
and his wife Josephine.

The house lies about ten miles to the west
of Paris. It was built by the Perrot family
during the second half of the seventeenth
century and was bought from them in the
1760s by a rich banker. For a time it was the
center of a fashionable society salon, but after
the French Revolution the family fell on hard
times and on 21 April 1799, Madame Josephine
Bonaparte took possession. She had lived at
neighboring Croissy with her first husband
Alexandre de Beauharnais, guillotined in 1794.
Two years after his death she married the
rising young general Bonaparte. After brilliant
successes in Italy he rose still higher, and in
May 1798 sailed for command in Egypt.
Before leaving he told Josephine that he
hoped to find her installed in a handsome
country house on his return; he also found

time on campaign to write to his brother
Joseph and his friend Bourienne asking them
to look out for a house for him. But it was
Josephine who made the choice; Malmaison
was near Paris–it was also in a district that she
already knew.

Cartloads of furniture, paintings, statuary
and objets d'art were soon making their way
to the little estate from Paris, so that during
the summer of 1799 the place began to return
to its old splendor. When, thanks to the
energy of his brother Julien, Napoleon was
created First Consul by the *coup d'état* of
Brumaire in November, Malmaison became
overnight the home of the first man in
France. This pleasant mansion, later nick-
named the Trianon Consulaire, now seemed
to some of his flatterers too modest a residence
for so great a man. For his part Napoleon
liked the house, and from 1799 to 1803
weekended there as often as possible. The
house parties of the First Consul and his wife
were alive with dancing, games and amateur
theatricals: these were years of happiness and
magnificence for Malmaison. From the beginning Josephine was the mistress of the
house. Her husband had urged on her the
strictest economy but in fact left her with a
virtually free hand. It was not long before he
too was ordering large modifications.

Josephine lavished improvements and em-
bellishments on the place and built up the art
collections with expert advice. She also initiated
plans to have it enlarged and redesigned

The Boudoir of the Empress Josephine at Malmaison.

inside and out in the fashionable neo-classical style, calling in the architects Charles Percier and Pierre François Fontaine, the self-appointed leaders of the new style in architecture. Josephine's patronage marked a turning point in their careers, for Napoleon was to appoint them chief government architects and entrust to them the development of the Empire style, but the commission at Malmaison was for them a refined purgatory.

First they were outraged by the fact that the First Consul proposed to live there at all; it was simply beneath his dignity. Next their professional ambitions were thwarted by the great man's parsimony. Having been refused permission to raze the place to the ground and build a grand new palace on the site, they compromised. Malmaison could be retained – only for servants' quarters and the lesser guest rooms, however. A new and palatial residence would still have to be built for the Consul himself. This plan too was vetoed, and for the next three years Percier and Fontaine struggled with a flood of instructions from their exasperating employers, which sometimes threatened the safety of the fabric and in any case, in the view of the architects, only toyed with the real problem. "We have been asked", they complained, "to renovate a poor house which is virtually in ruins and which was, in any case, originally built for a very commonplace type of person."

Walls were removed or repositioned so that the numerous living rooms of the original house could be opened out into spacious apartments. The entrance ante-chamber was enlarged to form a "vestibule of honor", while a second vestibule, tent-like in style, reflected the occupier's military profession. In a letter of March 1800, Napoleon called for the dining room to be enlarged and for extensions to the bedrooms; his own bedroom on the ground floor was to be transformed into a council chamber and he would move to the marriage chamber on the first floor. The new council room, with its décor of military trophies and the tenting ceiling and walls, was completed in two weeks. The decorations of a main reception room, including murals showing *Odin Receiving the Warriors of the Fatherland in Valhalla,* and *Ossian the Bard,* was done in a mere ten days.

The strange shape of the library is explained by the fact that Napoleon asked for it to be situated in a corner of the house which contained the flues of the kitchen chimneys. The Parisian cabinet maker, M. Jacob, solved the problem presented by the siting of the room and while commenting that the place looked more like the sacristry of a church than a library, Napoleon admired the ingenuity of the design. The work of architects and laborers can hardly have been helped by the fact that the First Consul continued to weekend at Malmaison throughout the alterations and watched their progress closely.

The gardens too were radically redesigned. The fashion for the English landscaped garden had swept France like the rest of Europe, and Josephine had the old formal gardens redesigned by a team first led by an Englishman named Howatson. The beautiful wooded walks and streams behind Malmaison today are the remains of this work.

After taking the title of emperor in 1804, Napoleon left Malmaison in favor of the former royal palace of Fontainebleau. Josephine was never at home in these new surroundings. When, in 1809, Napoleon repudiated his marriage with her to take Marie Louise of Austria to wife, she was allowed to live in retirement at Malmaison where she died in 1814.

Drottningholm, the summer residence of the Swedish monarchy, although sometimes referred to as the Swedish Versailles and, by comparison with the nearby Castle Gripsholm, built on a magnificent scale, is clearly a place for living in rather than for sheer ostentation. It stands in an idyllic setting on the island of Lövon in Lake Mälaren, not far from Stockholm. The name means "the Queen's Palace", and the original building (1581) was for Queen Catherine Jagellonica, the wife of John III of Sweden. It was destroyed by fire in 1661, and another queen, the Dowager Hedwig Eleonora, immediately called for plans for a new palace. They were drawn up by Nicodemus Tessin, Sweden's leading architect; after his death in 1681 the work was continued by his son, Nicodemus the Younger. The Tessin palace and its gardens were completed by 1700 but the low side wings were added in 1744 at the orders of Queen Ulricha. They are clearly modeled on Versailles.

Among the most impressive features of the palace is the majestic double staircase which occupies nearly a quarter of the main building. It announces that, for all its charm, Drottningholm is a royal residence and that for a time its owners were among the most powerful rulers in Europe. For 160 years Sweden has been neutral, but during the seventeenth and early eighteenth centuries she was a great military power. Among her warrior

kings was Charles X, Hedwig Eleonora's husband who died in 1660, and a whole gallery of paintings is devoted to his triumphs, while the Field Marshal's Hall contains the portraits of the great Charles XII (d.1718) and eighteen of his generals.

Court life at the palace reached its zenith during the reign of Gustavus III (1771–92), who was determined to restore a weakened royal power. Partly for reasons of political prestige he sought to emulate the splendors of Versailles, and the Gobelins Gallery contains tapestries given to him by his friend Louis XV of France. The magnificent little theater at Drottningholm was built during this period to house the court entertainments, which included some plays by the talented king himself. This theater and the one at Gripsholm are the only baroque theaters to have survived, and their elaborate stage machinery is not only fascinating for the layman but important to the historian of the theater. The theme of royal pomp is continued in the Ehrenstrahl Salon, lined with allegorical paintings of the history of the royal family by the German-born painter David von Ehrenstrahl (d. 1693), and there are many fine stucco ceilings. But the elegant library of Queen Ulricha, a rococo interior of white and gold, and the

Top *The baroque theater in the grounds of Drottningholm Palace.*

Above *The formal gardens in front of Drottningholm are typical of the baroque taste in garden design. The low wings, intended to give the original imposing but unpretentious palace the "Versailles look", were added in 1740.*

charming room of Hedwig Eleonora decorated blue and gold and used by Gustavus III as his bedroom, are achievements of elegant domestic interior design.

Gardens in the formal French style contain bronze statues taken as war booty during the seventeenth century from Prague and Fredriksborg in Denmark, whereas the English Garden, landscaped by F. M. Piper in the eighteenth century contains the charming little "Chinese pavilion". The Chinese-style silk for the furniture was woven in the hamlet of Kanton established by Queen Ulricha, following the European craze for *chinoiserie*. In this and many other ways Drottningholm reflects the changing fashions in royal life-style over two centuries.

The residences of royalty can hardly avoid

the grand scale but sometimes, as at Drottningholm, the mood of the place is one of civilized living rather than arrogant display. This is very much the case with **Hampton Court**, some ten miles from London, which seems patterned on the elegant comforts of the English country house. The first palace here was built by Cardinal Wolsey, Henry VIII's great minister. His court rivaled even that of the king; foreign embassies were entertained lavishly and so was King Henry and his retinue; a household staff of 500 waited on the Cardinal and nearly 300 guest rooms were kept constantly ready. Wolsey, who twice came close to being pope, was one of the great princes of Europe, and he naturally had enemies at court. They played on the king's jealousy of his overmighty friend, and although in 1528

Opposite *The summer palace of the Swedish monarchy, at Drottningholm outside Stockholm.*

Below *Little of the Tudor Hampton Court palace survives, but the main gateway and façade, shown here, date from the original palace of Cardinal Wolsey and King Henry VIII.*

Wolsey presented the sumptuous palace of Hampton to the king, he died two years later in poverty and disgrace.

The Great Gate House and the Base Court it leads to survive from Wolsey's palace, but much else was destroyed or modified by the royal architects. Henry VIII was an impatient patron: work on the Great Hall with its fine carvings and wooden hammer-beam roof was pressed on even at night in the glow of thousands of candles. Behind it at first-floor level is the Great Watching Chamber, the guard room for a group of spacious state rooms built for Henry but since destroyed. In the court beyond this lies the Chapel Royal, built by Wolsey and enriched with a fine wood vault by the king.

Hampton Court was used by the Tudors and Stuarts and by Lord Protector Cromwell, but during the reign of James II it fell into neglect. But the year after his fall in 1688, the joint monarchs William III and Mary II commissioned Sir Christopher Wren to plan a new palace there which was to outshine even Versailles. His first designs, which involved the destruction of the Tudor buildings except for the Great Hall, were lively and vigorous, but they were rejected. Perhaps, as one art historian has suggested, they failed to capture that "regal monotony of the Park Front at Versailles". More restrained designs were prepared but in fact shortage of funds meant that only part of these could be fulfilled. As a result the regal scale of Hampton Court is not massed by excessive ostentation.

Wren had to plan for two sets of state rooms,

77

one set each for the joint monarchs. They form wings on the east and south sides of the Fountain Court at the back of the palace. The handsomely proportioned rooms are decorated with some fine carvings by Grinling Gibbons and paintings by Tintoretto, Titian, Veronese and Correggio. From the King's suite can be seen the Privy Garden, closed off from the river by a magnificent wrought-iron screen originally designed for the Great Fountain Garden. Behind this is the landing stage where the royal barge was moored, ready to take the king to London. The Queen's apartments look over the Broad Walk to the Great Fountain Garden. The fountain is set in a large semi-circular lawn, bounded by an ornamental canal and crossed by three tree-lined avenues radiating from the central entrance on the east front of the palace.

On the north side of the palace lies the indoor Real Tennis court built for Henry VIII, and beyond that the Wilderness, a favorite feature of Tudor Gardens where formality gives way to a more natural landscape. Here the famous Hampton Court Maze was planted at the end of the seventeenth century.

The great house at **Compton Wynyates** in Warwickshire always takes the visitor by surprise. It lies deep in the English countryside away from the main roads and is in any case

Top *The water garden at Hampton Court.*

Above *The Tudor Great Hall at Hampton Court, built for King Henry VIII.*

difficult to find. Approached for the first time on a misty January day, its magical cluster of chimneys and rambling roofs rises out of the wooded hollow in which the house is set like some fairyland township. Even at the height of the summer, when the brick-work glows red against the green of the lawn and the darker wooded slope behind, one is never quite prepared for the way the drive dips sharply down and, all mystery gone, the great mansion lies like the home of some P. G. Wodehouse idyll.

The house we see today is largely the work of Sir William Compton, Squire of the Body to King Henry VIII, though there had been a manor house on the site since the twelfth century. The surprise impact of the place derives partly from the fact that while it lies in a district of limestone buildings, this house was built in brick. Until the fifteenth century, this was a material comparatively rare in England, but campaigns in the Hundred Years War introduced the English gentry to the brick châteaux of France. By the 1500s the craze for brick spread across England irrespective of the natural materials of the various districts and counties. It was versatile and vivid, and different colored bricks could be used in decorative designs known as diaper work. There are examples of this at Compton

Wynyates, and also of half-timbering, another favorite device with Tudor architects.

It is a big house, solidly built, yet the great structure seems full of movement. The roofs seen rising one behind the other from the high ground at the wrought-iron entrance gates first give the impression. The tower of the inner courtyard and the chimneys emphasize it. Then the gables create an unexpected effect. The right one seems to be set forward and the left one back from the main façade until one realizes that while the herringbone design of the half-timbering in both is identical, the gable on the right is larger than the other. The strangely squat porch is set off center and emphasizes the contrived asymmetry of the design, the windows are of varying sizes and are placed at slightly staggered intervals above one another. A moat once surrounded the house, and its reflections would have heightened the effect of optical illusion to a startling degree. Now a fine English lawn spreads out before the mansion and to one side; beyond it there is a formal garden and a topiary of clipped hedges, shaped into birds and geometric designs. Beyond again is a little ditch or "ha-ha" which separates the gardens from the rough pasture beyond and the animals that graze there.

Compton Wynyates is a far cry from the

Looking down on the great Tudor house of Compton Wynyates across the topiary hedge garden at the side of the house.

stern fortifications of Krak des Chevaliers or Château Gaillard, yet the moat was only part decorative. The mansion was built only a generation after King Henry VII had fought his way to the crown of England and men could not be sure that the civil strife we call the Wars of the Roses was over for good. It was a time when the rich did well to make their homes a little castle-like. The mansion in Warwickshire is even more remote from the mood of the great baroque palaces and the haughty grandeur of Versailles. Set among the woods and surrounded by the rich agricultural land that paid the lord his rents, it is a parable of privilege in a land of plenty. The architecture is that of the house rather than the palace, but the scale and the luxury of the place are truly palatial. In common with all the buildings in this book it is a symbol of wealth and power; ironically the bastions of the power and privilege of the past have become the treasured beauties of the present.